Student Achievement Through Staff Development

Bruce Joyce
Beverly Showers

Longman
New York & London

Student Achievement Through Staff Development

Longman Inc., 95 Church Street, White Plains, N. Y. 10601

Associated companies:
Longman Group Ltd., London
Longman Cheshire Pty., Melbourne
Longman Paul Pty., Auckland
Copp Clark Pitman, Toronto
Pitman Publishing Inc., New York

Senior editor: Naomi Silverman
Text design: Steven Krastin
Cover design: Charlene Felker
Production supervisor: Judi Stern
Compositor: Harris Educational Consultants
Printer: Malloy Lithographing Inc.

Library of Congress Cataloging-in-Publication Data

Joyce, Bruce R.
    Student achievement through staff development.

    Bibliography: p.
    Includes index.
    1. Teachers — In-service training — United States.
2. Continuing education — United States. 3. Career
development — United States. 4. Academic achievement.
I. Showers, Beverly. II. Title.
LB1731.J69 1988   371.1'46   87-3052
ISBN 0-582-28409-0 (pbk.)
88 89 90 91 92 93   9 8 7 6 5 4 3 2 1

Dedication

to Reuben and Modean Short

and

their affection for

Seamus Joyce

HOW MANY DO YOU NEED TO SEE?

How many effective schools would you have to see to be persuaded of the educability of all children? If your answer is more than one, then I submit that you have reasons of your own for preferring to believe that basic pupil performance derives from family background instead of school response to family background. Whether or not we will ever effectively teach the children of the poor is probably far more a matter of politics than of social science, and that is as it should be.

We can, whenever and wherever we want, successfully teach all children whose schooling is of interest to us. We already know more than we need to do that. Whether or not we do it must depend on how we feel about the fact that we haven't so far.

Ron Edmonds

TABLE OF CONTENTS

We propose the establishment of a staff development system designed to ensure that education personnel are in continuous high states of growth. Training research and research on teaching and learning have reached the stage where a system that increases student aptitude, achievement, and personal and social development can be designed with confidence.

The proposed system of staff development offers service to individual, school, and district-sponsored initiatives for school improvement. The condition of the school is the key to effective programs for individual and system initiatives as well as for those designed to generate more effective curriculum and instruction for the school itself.

The development of an environment in which the continual improvement of curriculum and instruction has a central place is critical. Each year the faculty selects one or two areas as a common focus. Study teams, peer coaching teams, and an active leadership council tend the social system and keep it lively and cohesive.

Chapter Four

Student learning is the criterion for the selection of the content for staff development. We examine research on the effects of various options on academic, social and personal goals. These include the development of the aptitude to learn, the mastery of academic skills, information, and concepts, social learning, and the improvement of self-image and moral commitment.

Chapter Five

We present a framework for organizing the content of the three substanive components of the system. The individual, school, and systemic components need to be oriented toward changes in practice that offer promise for student growth in the personal, social, and academic domains.

Chapter Six

Based on research on how education personnel acquire teaching skills and strategies and the dynamics of school change, staff development programs can be designed for a high probability of success. The research is reviewed and its application is illustrated with a variety of programs including the development of simple but important skills and the acquisition of repertoires of teaching models.

Chapter Seven

The building blocks of the system are study groups of teachers who work together to master new content, teaching processes, and to improve elements of the social climate of the school. The development and the operation of these groups is the substance of this chapter. The processes of peer study and coaching are illustrated through examples of programs designed for individuals and school and district initiatives.

Chapter Eight

The Nature of the Skills Underlying "Good Practice"   95

Educational practices require both knowledge and the skills to use them. The "invisible" skills of teaching are the thought processes involved in planning and in interaction with the students. Learning to nurture students as they respond to unfamiliar cognitive and social tasks involves new ways of processing information while teaching.

Chapter Nine

Evaluating Staff Development Programs   111

The evaluation of staff development involves documenting chains of events. The variables include the characteristics of the participants, the character of the schools in which they work, the components of programs and the degrees to which they are implemented, the knowledge and skills that result, and the effects on students. Categories of variables are described with the instruments for measuring them. Designs for evaluating a variety of types of programs are provided.

Chapter Ten

The States of Growth of People in the Organization   129

Although attitudes of personnel toward particular staff development offerings are important, the general disposition of people toward their environments greatly affects responses to training. A general description of orientations toward growth is provided along with discussion of the contribution of psychological maturity, self concept, and conceptual flexibility.

Chapter Eleven

Buying Time   145

Embedding staff development in the workplace involves finding time for the study of teaching and the curriculum. We present a number of low cost and costless ways of freeing personnel for coaching and training.

Chapter Twelve

We present a sample policy statement for a district that wishes to develop the three-dimensional system that we have proposed. The elements of the statement are accompanied by a rationale of the type that might be presented to policy makers.

Chapter Thirteen

Integrated approaches to staff development and preservice preparation will enhance both. We discuss the redesign of preservice teacher education with special emphasis on preparation for life-long learning.

Coda

We believe that a strong staff development system can be developed within the current organization and within current fiscal resources. The key may be the aspiration to have much more effective schools and the will to bring about much stronger staff development for all personnel.

Acknowledgments

Our wonderful colleagues in thought and action have provided ideas and opportunity to test them in action. Michael Fullan, Carol and Bill Mell, Morgan Hulett, Dan Howe, Ray Beard, Barrie Bennett, Carol Rolheiser-Bennett, David Hunt, and recently Carlene and Joe Murphy.

Ken Harris of Harris Educational Consultants, Eugene, Oregon has provided the knowledge and skill to allow the production of this book to move electronically from word processing to programs to organize data for publishing, and finally the production of camera ready copy. He prepared the copy on a Cordata ATD-8 computer, using Xerox Desktop Publishing Series: Ventura Publisher Edition, and a Cordata LP300X Laser printer. His competence and patience are greatly appreciated by author and publishers alike.

Naomi Silverman is a wonderful editor.

Beverly Showers
Bruce Joyce
Booksend Laboratories
Eugene, Oregon

PREFACE

Writing a book is not always an enjoyable experience, but writing this one has been a pleasure and a great source of meaning for us. Much of the pleasure has come from thinking about and revisiting so many old friends. Some of these friends are books and their authors. Others are reports of research and their investigators. Many are places where we have worked and people we have trained and studied and who, more important for this enterprise, have informed and trained us in turn. The ideas given us by our mentors with the right of unrestricted use have been blended with our reading and our experience to bring us to the place where we can make bold with these ideas.

Our product is a platform for thinking about and strengthening the investment that must be made in education personnel. Thus, it is a rationale and general outline of the policies we think will enhance schools and our children. For student learning is the center of this profession's work. And, while staff development in education will surely benefit its personnel, the professional function of the educator's growth is the growth of children.

Educational research, badly funded and difficult to conduct, has progressed slowly but in recent years has reached a new stage of development. Information is available about how teaching, schooling, and curriculum can be organized to accelerate student learning and the aptitude to learn further. Knowledge about innovation in education, the conduct of curricular change, and the processes by which educators learn new skills and knowledge and use them, all these have matured greatly within the last decade.

Thus this book does not celebrate current staff development practices, although it acknowledges and builds on them. Rather, it presses toward a future in which the investment in teachers and administrators will be adequate and time for study will be part of their work. As that investment increases, the opportunity exists for research and clinical experience to be used as the basis for the selection of the goals of staff development and the processes used to achieve them.

What students bring to school greatly affects the learning that will take place. Their social context powerfully influences their opportunities to participate in their culture and to use what education brings them. In a positive sense, the job of the educator is to compete with the student and the society by increasing the talents of learning and the humanizing dimensions of social experience. The purpose of staff development is to increase the ability of teachers to engage in that competition.

Bruce Joyce and Beverly Showers
Eugene, Oregon
New Years Day, 1987

CHAPTER ONE

HUMAN RESOURCE DEVELOPMENT AS THE GOAL

As this is written, the field of staff development is evolving gradually from a patchwork of courses and workshops into a system ensuring that education professionals regularly enhance their academic knowledge and professional performance. States, school districts, intermediate agencies, and teachers' organizations are searching for ways to enlarge the investment in staff development and generate better forms of it. They are trying to develop a system that will embed professional growth opportunities into the work life of teachers and administrative and supervisory personnel. Research on the knowledge and skills of teachers is increasing rapidly and the study of programs and designs is maturing.

The focus of this book is on the planning of a comprehensive system and the governance, design, and implementation of specific programs within that system. Much of the book consists of recommendations that are based on the study of a wide range of staff development programs, research on teachers and teaching, information about the workplace, research on how teachers learn and ideas about how to design effective programs. The authors have accumulated and organized the research on staff development and teaching, conducted studies on training, studied several dozen staff development programs, organized research on more than 3,000 teachers (including case studies of about 400) and conducted staff development programs for several thousand teachers and administrators. They have helped approximately 100 agencies plan programs, including several states, many districts, a few teacher organizations, and a couple of foreign countries.

One of the net results of this experience is a sense not only of what is known but what is not known, and the reader will find that there are many important issues that need thoughtful attention and careful research.

Research and clinical study are not the only bases on which we can plan comprehensive systems. In fact, even the best-designed research needs interpretation and evaluation if it is to be applied to policymaking. A number of the more important assumptions should be made clear at the outset. In the sections that deal with policy we will base our recommendations on a combination of information and these assumptions.

ASSUMPTIONS

First is the belief that we should develop comprehensive resource-development systems for education personnel. We will argue that the institutions that employ educators have the responsibility to ensure that all personnel regularly study teaching, school improvement, and academic substance. As we discuss the workplace we will emphasize that the original task-assignments of teachers and administrators neglected to include time to prepare for teaching, for the study of teaching, for cooperative efforts in school improvement, or for academic study. These issues were simply not built into the job. The implicit assumption was that preservice teacher education provided all the knowledge and skill that one would need throughout the career. Salary incentives and recertification requirements were used to induce teachers to return to school for courses, workshops, and institutes, but the responsibility for further study was largely that of the individual. Essentially, if the incentives failed to work the practitioner was unsupported. The response to the opportunities provided by universities and other agencies has varied widely. Some persons responded early in their careers, attending a number of courses to achieve a permanent certificate or reach a certain point on the salary scale and then did not engage in further voluntary activity for more than 20 years.

We believe that the study of academic substance, teaching, and school improvement should be an inescapable part of the job and that the organization should arrange and pay for the system that ensures that formal study is an important component of the job of teaching. We think that incentives are not a good substitute for the embedding of staff development support within the context of the workplace.

Education is the only complex occupation where institutions have been ambivalent about providing continuing education for their employees. We believe that ambivalence should end and that agencies should take responsibility for the academic and clinical health of their personnel.

Second is the assumption that student learning can be greatly increased through human resource programs. While an important reason for staff development is to benefit the personnel themselves, organizations invest in comprehensive programs to develop the skills and knowledge of their personnel to enable that organization to reach its objectives. In the case of education there are two interrelated broad goals. The first is to enable the students to learn the information, skills, concepts, and values that comprise the curriculum. The second is to increase the students' ability to learn in the future.

We believe that research on teaching and learning has resulted in a considerable array of curricular and instructional alternatives that have great promise for increasing student learning (chapter four). These include a large number of models of teaching that have a strong research base under them (Joyce & Weil, 1986) and a much clearer picture of the things that more effective teachers do to plan and carry out instructional programs for their students (Walberg, 1986).

The potential is great. Many researched teaching strategies have enough power to help the average student (the student normally at the 50th percentile) achieve what the top 10 percent of students normally achieve, and can help the students who usually achieve in the lower and upper quartiles make comparable gains in rate of learning.

The fundamental task of teaching is to help the students "look good" as learners — that is, to help them behave with confidence and skill. The tools now exist which will provide the means whereby any faculty can help its students look as good as or even better than the students in our highest-achieving schools.

Third, recent research on staff development has demonstrated that virtually all teachers can learn the most powerful and complex teaching strategies provided that staff development is designed properly. We are in a position where curricula and models of teaching that are now rarely employed by teachers can be learned and used by them (Joyce & Showers, 1983; chap. 8). Research on curriculum implementation and staff development has demonstrated that difficulties in implementation and the low frequency of use of the more powerful teaching strategies has been a product of weak preservice and inservice programs, not in the learning ability of teachers.

Fourth, the norms of the workplace of teaching — the school — need to change if powerful staff development is to be implemented; reciprocally, when it is implemented, the energy of the workplace increases considerably. Teachers and administrators have worked in relatively isolated environments (Lortie, 1975) and faculties have had relatively little experience in cooperative planning of school improvement or staff development programs. Effective staff development requires cooperative relationships that break down the isolation and increase the collective strength of the community of educators who staff the school.

Fifth, embedded staff development will have a great effect on the ethos of the profession of education — the beliefs and behavior of the professional community. Currently teachers have to rely on their personal knowledge of teaching for most of their decisions. The products of formal research and study of teaching are unknown to many of them and few have had the opportunity either to study formal knowledge or to learn how to make it work in the classroom. A strong system of preservice and inservice education will have a great effect by providing common knowledge and the skills to use it.

Finally, we will stress throughout that professional knowledge consists of three overlapping components: the study of academic content, that which undergirds the content that is to be learned by the students; the study of curricular and instructional strategies, the process of organizing content and helping students study it; and the process of school improvement, the cooperative work by faculties to make the school better (Joyce & Clift, 1983). The school has its impact in three ways: one is what is taught, the second is in how it is taught, and the third is its social environment. Teachers and administrators need to be engaged in the continuous study of all three, continually increasing knowledge of academic content, models of teaching, and models for school environments and how to create them.

SUMMARY

The pages that follow are organized around the design of a staff development system that pervades the school and is the responsibility of the organization. The system will be built on research on how teachers and administrators learn and how to design effective programs within an embedded system of staff development. The powerful teaching strategies and curricula that have been developed over the last two decades need to be available to all personnel. The major goal is to increase student learning; however, side effects will include great changes in the workplace by increasing the study of teaching and learning and supporting communities of faculty members working together for their students.

CHAPTER TWO

A PERVASIVE SYSTEM

In this chapter we describe what a comprehensive system of human resource development might look like in education – the kinds of services it would be designed to render, provisions for governance, personnel, and organization, and how it might be used to serve individual teachers, faculties in the service of school improvement, and district initiatives in curriculum, instruction, and technology.

To ensure that education personnel are in continuous growth is our goal. The idea seems innocuous enough. Given the awesome responsibilities of educating the young and the rapid changes in knowledge and social conditions of the times, creating environments that enable teachers to be continuously supported in a high state of growth seems like an obvious and natural thing to do. Yet, the creation of a system that will achieve this is in fact a radical innovation in schooling, and an extremely difficult one. The increase in staff development time will in itself constitute a major change. As this is written, the average teacher in the United States engages in the formal study of teaching and schooling, including new content and curriculums, for only about three days per year (Howey, Yarger, & Joyce, 1978) and has conferences with supervisors only two or three times each year. The system we envision would provide 15 or 20 days of study each year and teachers would visit each other regularly to work cooperatively on polishing their skills and adding to them.

Many policy makers, principals, and teachers find the idea of a comprehensive staff development system somewhat foreign and even anxiety-producing. Many board of education members and some superintendents, when approached for increased staff development budgets, appear to be surprised that the organization should engage in substantial efforts to ensure the academic and clinical health of its personnel. They have viewed continued learning as the province of the individual

5

practitioner. We would persuade them to embrace the responsibility on behalf of the organization.

Many teachers and principals are not charmed by the idea, either. These people have come to enjoy the autonomy of the classroom and some regard supervision or required staff development as an intrusion on their self-supervised work. We would also persuade them otherwise. Reaching agreement that a system is needed may be the most difficult part of the building process.

PURPOSES

We suggest that there are three general purposes to be served and around which strands of the system can be organized.

Enhancement of Individual Clinical Skills and Academic Knowledge

One purpose is to ensure that all practitioners, teachers, and administrators are continuously polishing and expanding their current repertoires of knowledge and skill throughout their careers. Knowledge and skill are important, and neither are automatically enhanced. Adding new content and teaching strategies to the existing repertoire to the point where they can be used effectively in the instructional setting has turned out to be difficult and requires very hard work. (See chapter six for the research on which this assertion is based.)

The Study of School Improvement

While the most familiar image of teachers and administrators is at work as individuals, the improvement of the environment of the school requires collective work (Joyce, Hersh, & McKibbin, 1983; Fullan, 1983). The social climate of the school and the attitudes and patterns of behavior it promotes greatly influence the process of education. For example, rigorous standards are promoted not so much by what individuals do as what the faculty does as a whole. A teacher who works alone to impose standards not promoted by the faculty as a whole is in for a very frustrating and largely ineffectual experience. The second purpose of a comprehensive system is to unite the staffs of schools in studying ways of improving the school and engagement in continuous programs to make it better. Schools become outstanding when school improvement is prominent among their features. Schools whose programs are neglected become less effective quite rapidly.

District-wide Initiatives to Improve the Educational Program

The classroom and the school exist in the context of the larger agency that has responsibility for curriculum development and implementation and the allocation of resources for facilities and technologies. Curriculum improvement and the introduction of new technologies require extensive study and training if they are to be implemented successfully. The human resource development system needs to serve the policies of the district regarding curriculum and technology, ensuring that they are effectively used.

RATIONALE

As Fullan (1982) has pointed out so carefully, an innovation is not sustained unless there is a shared understanding of its purposes, rationale, and processes. Underlying the three purposes that a comprehensive system should serve is a compelling rationale. It is based on realities in common practice, combined with research and the development of new ideas and procedures.

Supporting the Continuous Study of Teaching and Learning

There is a considerable reservoir of effective teaching skills and strategies *that are virtually unknown to most of today's practitioners* (chapter four). The currently weak system of staff development does not bring these to the attention of teachers and administrators and does not include training designed to ensure that those strategies are mastered and used (chapters four and five). Yet, programs can be designed to include procedures that will enable virtually any current practitioner to develop high levels of skill with them. We have confidence that during the next few years there will be an even greater increase in knowledge about effective teaching than we have had during the past twenty years. There is a belief in some quarters that experience in teaching and administering will by itself result in knowledge and skill equal to the products of research and development. This is simply not true. The most gifted practitioners recognize this and are the most eager to see the development of a system to bring these powerful tools within their reach. In fact, most practitioners acknowledge the need. Thus, the rationale for the first goal is that there is much to learn and the means for doing so are at hand.

Supporting Faculty Study
of School Improvement

The reality is that the school climate is developed through collective action, that there is considerable knowledge about the dimensions of the climate that enhance learning, and that the isolation of practitioners in what Lortie (1975) has called the "cellular" nature of the school has prevented faculties from acting collectively to study what works and how to possess it. The nature of the school has caused most teachers and administrators to concentrate on the instructional and leadership skills that they can employ alone rather than on the skills that are employed in close cooperation with other people (Goodlad, 1984). Coherent curriculums and social systems, however, are made by communities of people, and the tools are available to help faculties plan collective action, however (Fullan & Park, 1981; Fullan, Miles, & Taylor, 1980; Schmuck, Runkel, Arends, & Arends 1977).

Supporting District Initiatives
in Curriculum and Technology

The implementation of curricular and technological changes is virtually impossible without very strong staff development (Fullan, 1982; Goodlad & Klein, 1970; Joyce, Hersh, & McKibbin, 1983). Curricular change involves innovations in content and instructional processes and materials. The current staff development system is too weak to support curriculum change beyond a simple change in textbooks in all but a handful of school districts (Fullan & Pomfret, 1977). Technological change is in the same situation. Even common media like film, videotape, and broadcast television are almost unused in schools, despite their enormous educational value. The computer comes late and lumbering to our schools. Initiatives like mainstreaming of handicapped students have labored dreadfully, denying the children full benefits (SRI International, 1983).

Again, research has progressed to the point where the knowledge exists to engineer staff development programs on behalf of curricular and technological initiative at the district level. Our intent is to empower individuals, faculties, and district policy makers equally through human resource development.

DIMENSIONS OF A COMPREHENSIVE SYSTEM

The system that we visualize is not particularly complex, although in large education units the logistics can exercise the best managerial skills.

However, creating the system requires a many-sided effort. The core is the development of many small communities of teachers and administrators carefully linked within and across schools and supported by human and material resources.

Study Groups and Coaching Teams: Building Communities of Learners

Each teacher and administrator has membership in a team whose members support one another in study. For example, each person can have membership in a coaching team of two or three. Each team is linked to one or two others, forming a study group of no more than six members. The principal and the leaders of the study groups in a school form the staff development/school improvement council of that school. A representative from each school within a district cluster (usually a high school and its feeder schools) serves on the District Cluster Network Committee, which coordinates staff development efforts between schools and the district and works directly with the director of staff development (see Figure 1).

Figure 1. A District Staff Development Governance Structure

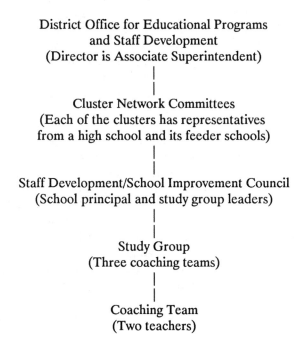

District Office for Educational Programs
and Staff Development
(Director is Associate Superintendent)
|
|
Cluster Network Committees
(Each of the clusters has representatives
from a high school and its feeder schools)
|
|
Staff Development/School Improvement Council
(School principal and study group leaders)
|
|
Study Group
(Three coaching teams)
|
|
Coaching Team
(Two teachers)

This governance structure is illustrated by the staff at the Onyx Elementary School, whose faculty numbers thirty-six. One teacher, Adrienne, has a coaching partner, Katherine. They belong to Study Group A, which has six members. Adrienne is, with five others, a member of the Onyx School staff development council. She and the principal are members of the cluster network committee, which consists of representatives from one high school, two middle schools, and six elementary schools in the Opal district.

Through a council of teachers and administrators, that cluster, with the three others in the district, is linked to the district Office for Educational Programs and Staff Development. The director of that Office is an associate superintendent and reports directly to the superintendent

The coaching teams and study groups are the building blocks of the system. Team members support one another as they study academic content and teaching skills and strategies. The study groups within each school are responsible for implementing school improvement efforts and district-wide initiatives. In chapters six and seven we will discuss those activities in some detail.

Governance: Three Types of Operation

The comprehensive staff development system is designed to generate three kinds of effort. One is that each practitioner will be regularly engaged in the study of some aspect of academic content or clinical skill. We refer to this as the *individual* component, because the product is to be manifested in the individual's clinical competence as an instructor. Second is that the faculty will be refining or renovating some aspect of the school program. We refer to this as the *collective* component, because it requires the cooperative enterprise of the school faculty. Third is that a district-wide initiative in curriculum or technology will be in some stage of implementation. We refer to this as the *systemic* component, because it requires coordinated effort among the members of all branches of the district organization. In Adrienne's case, her study group is exploring how to organize their students into cooperative learning groups (Slavin, 1983; Johnson & Johnson, 1979). They have attended a workshop and are helping one another put into practice what they have learned. The Onyx School's Improvement Initiative for the year is focused on an attempt to develop a more affirmative climate for the students and to increase the amount of cooperative study they engage in, both in and out of school. They have based their effort on research showing that an affirmative school climate and increased study, especially cooperative study, are related to student learning. Third, the district initiative for a two-year period focuses on increased use of the computer for instruction in writing. The Onyx school has combined this with their own effort to increase independent and cooperative study.

How are the three components governed? Two levels of decisions are to be made. One is about participation and the other is about the provision of support personnel and materials. In the case of the clinical component, all teachers and administrators are expected to be engaged in the study of at least one aspect of academic content or teaching skill or strategy. Each individual can select the type of study to be engaged in during any year, but the selections have to be feasible in terms of resources and support. For example, a physics teacher may decide to study some aspect of physics, but cannot do so unless the means are available (e.g., a course on high-temperature physics cannot be taken unless it is available). The district staff development committee is responsible for collecting suggestions from the schools, study groups, coaching teams, and individuals and generating the program of offerings that will be supported during any given year. The program will be balanced so that individuals receive support for their first choices fairly regularly. The committee is responsible also for educating their colleagues to the possibilities. The faculty cannot choose teaching strategies that they have not heard of, so the committee seeks to develop increasingly sophisticated bases for choice.

Similarly, the school committees make choices for the collective component and the district committee tries to support the choices that are made for the school foci and, when possible, to integrate district initiatives with those of the schools. There may be expertise among the district personnel, or consultants may be engaged. In some cases, members of a faculty may travel to receive instruction about the innovation and how to make it work.

The focus for systemic component is selected by the district committee after study of the alternatives. It is extremely important that the focus be narrowed as much as possible and backed up by adequate training. In the past many districts have diffused their staff development programs by selecting too many initiatives for adequate support to be mustered to ensure implementation for any of them.

THE SUPPORT SUBSYSTEM

Each of the components depends for support on training and study opportunities. The components do not so much require different kinds of training and consultatory help as they do different patterns for accomplishing their ends.

The Individual Component

The individual component requires patterns of courses, workshops, and consultant services to enable individuals and coaching teams to study some aspect of teaching and to enhance their skills. Adrienne and Katherine have chosen to work as a team and selected cooperative learning from a set of alternatives that included offerings from the following categories:

ACADEMIC COURSES

For elementary teachers these included courses in mechanics, literature (contemporary poetry), children's literature, the geography of Africa, and a variety of other subjects.

Workshops on Teaching

There are several levels of study (introductions and advanced study) on a variety of subjects. Cooperative learning includes three levels of topics. In addition to three levels on cooperative learning strategies, the offerings include several models of teaching (concept learning, inductive teaching, synectics, memory models, etc.), several offerings on lesson design (Hunter, 1981) and a series on classroom management for beginning teachers. In addition, there are workshops on teaching each of the core elementary school subjects. This year there is an extensive series on the teaching of writing.

Workshops on the Study of the Student

Each year there are workshops on two different ways of looking at the learning styles of students and the design of instruction to maximize strengths and help students strengthen their weaknesses. This year there is a course on self-concept and one on developmental psychology.

Workshops on Technology

There is an extensive series on the use of the computer, a set of short workshops on television and video recording, and photography. The courses and workshops are offered in a number of ways. Some are distance-based courses offered from the state university, which use readings, broadcast television, and television recordings as instructional modes. A larger number are workshops taught by district personnel. A few are taught by university personnel who come to the district on a regular basis.

The Collective Component

The offerings to support the collective component are similar to the ones offered under the clinical component except that they have been requested by particular school faculties and are offered for the faculty as a whole. Also, there are workshops on the study of schools thought to be effective schools and the process of school improvement.

The personnel who offer the workshops are available to the school for on-site consultation on the topics they teach. Whenever qualified district personnel are available, they teach the courses.

The Systemic Component

The systemic component, being district-wide, is a more complex operation. A cadre of administrators and teachers representing each school study the initiative for a year and conduct many of the in-school offerings connected with the innovation. University personnel and consultants provide the training for the cadre and work with them as they provide workshops and other support for their peers. The study groups and peer coaching teams provide assistance to their members as the difficult process of implementing the initiative takes place.

Thus, every person in the district has responsibility for cooperating with the systemic and collective foci and for developing a program for personal growth, possibly in conjunction with a peer coaching partner or a study group.

THE SUPPORT CADRE

An essential component of an effective system is personnel who can offer instruction and support to others in the areas that are under study. These persons need to develop a very high level of competence in an area to the point where they can deal with its theory, demonstrate it, organize practice with it, and help coaching teams and study groups sustain its use in the instructional setting. There needs to be a relatively small group of specialists in curriculum and instruction who study the alternatives, study staff development and school improvement, and organize the offerings that support each of the three substantive components. We can refer to these persons as *staff development specialists.*

In addition, as areas are selected for study, instructional teams made up of teachers and administrators with an interest in the area need to be organized into *instructional teams* who will offer the instruction and support on specific topics. For example, if inductive teaching is selected, the instructional team would study its theory, practice it with students, and prepare demonstrations for use in workshops and courses. Because it takes time to develop competence to the point where one can offer instruction to others, the instructional team should be selected a year before any offerings are to be made in the area, so that they have ample time for preparation. From whom do they receive guidance? If there are already qualified district personnel, then they should be utilized. If not, consultants may have to be utilized or the team may have to travel to a setting where they can study the innovation, such as a university, an institute, an extended series of workshops, or a district that has made much use of the content.

The important feature is that the system include a commitment to the development of in-house competence wherever feasible, relying on external consultants primarily to build the capability of the within-district personnel.

Returning to Adrienne for an example, she and Katherine are members of an instructional team that specializes in the use of the teaching strategy *synectics* for the teaching of writing. During the year they will offer a series of workshops, as part of the collective component, to the faculty of an elementary school that has chosen writing as its school improvement thrust for the year.

Even where offerings are distance-based or staffed primarily by external personnel, an instructional team needs to be organized to provide leadership for the individuals, coaching teams, study groups, and faculties who are participants. In fact, during the first year or two that a topic is supported, the instructional team might work with the external personnel as co-trainers while they develop their competence to generate offerings without outside support.

SUMMARY

The proposed system is straightforward. Its organizational building blocks include coaching teams combined into study groups within faculties that are networked within clusters of schools. Its three components serve individuals, faculties, and the system as a whole. The governance structure provides for teacher, administrator, and policy-maker participation at all levels of decisionmaking. Support offerings are selected carefully on a basis of careful study of the alternatives and perceived needs of personnel. Offerings are probably fewer than in many operating systems but are in depth. Within-district personnel are heavily utilized as training teams to the point where as many as 1 out of 10 teachers and administrators is serving as an instructor at any given time.

As we will see, leadership at all levels is vital to the development of the system. The broad governance structure ensures that ideas and energy from the teaching and administrative corps are driving forces. The energy and dedication of the district, cluster, and school committees are essential elements, and the personnel designated to lead and coordinate those committees need to be real students of the field as well as capable organizers.

CHAPTER THREE

THE SYNERGETIC SCHOOL

The social organization of the school is critical to the success not only of staff development initiatives that are addressed to the school (the collective dimension) but those that are addressed to individuals (the clinical dimension) and system policy (the systemic dimension) as well. The reasons are not difficult to fathom, but in practice many otherwise promising staff development efforts have faltered and even failed completely because insufficient attention has been paid to the development of a social organization that is congenial to change and growth (Little, 1982). As we will see, training to reach an adequate level of competence in new skills and knowledge requires intensive study, many demonstrations, and opportunities for practice in the training setting. To elevate the new learning to the point where it can be used effectively in the instructional setting, teachers and administrators have to engage in extensive practice. Both the training and the practice have to reside comfortably in the school setting and be collaborative activities – personnel have to provide much assistance to one another during the early stages of practice with unfamiliar skills and knowledge.

Because past staff development systems have been relatively weak, the establishment of effective programs – ones that enable teachers to strengthen existing knowledge and skills significantly and to add fresh knowledge and instructional models to their repertoire – has to be regarded as innovative (Joyce, Hersh, & McKibbin, 1983; Fullan, 1982; and Miles & Huberman, 1984). As Fullan has carefully pointed out, it is shared understandings that sustain an innovation. All personnel need to study the innovation and the innovative process thoroughly and develop the common knowledge that will guide their collective behavior. The activities depicted in the scenario in the previous chapter are examples. When Adrienne selects a workshop and attends it, she needs the support of her study team and coaching partners in order to practice the skills she has learned until they become a smooth and powerful part of her repertoire. When the school selects its focus for the year, the faculty needs to work together both to select the goals and to engage in the process for achieving them. When the district selects the area that will receive its attention the school has to be organized so that the innovation can be understood and the faculty cooperates in ensuring that they receive appropriate training and profit from it. All of these need a shared understanding of the nature of the system, the purposes of the three dimensions, the nature of training and how to profit from it, and the determination to work for the common cause so that all of the initiatives pay off.

The necessity for collective decision making and collaborative activity requires changes in the traditional relationships among teachers and between teachers and administrators. As Lortie (1975) has so eloquently pointed out, teaching has been conducted in relative isolation. In most settings teachers rarely observe one another teach and are seen by administrators rarely, in many cases only two or three times a year. The time for preparation of instruction is meager, as is time for the meetings that are necessary to discuss the state of the school and curriculum and instruction. In the course of adapting to the isolation many teachers have worked out comfortable patterns of behavior that fit the isolated conditions and the low degree of collaborative action that characterize the workplace. Essentially, teachers have learned to work alone, relying on themselves, unentangled by group decisions or the necessity to coordinate activities with others. The development of the conditions that will sustain effective training requires great changes in the normative behavior patterns that have developed over the years. Teaching becomes more public, decisions become collective and thus more complicated, connections with administrators become closer and more reciprocal, and some of these changes cause temporary discomfort that is alleviated only by still greater contact with others.

The research we can draw on to understand how the social organization can facilitate staff development is now substantial (Fullan, 1982). Rather than reviewing it formally we have distilled it into a series of propositions on which we believe healthy school organizations can be built and sustained. None of these propositions are mysterious, nor do any of them require virtuosic levels of skill. Yet, each of them requires changes in practice and in the norms of the workplace and, hence, effort must be expended to deal with the anxiety that is contemplated during any change process. Adopting new behaviors is not nearly as difficult or aggravating as giving up or modifying familiar behaviors, and we need to make the process palatable. Yet, we reiterate, the new behaviors are not difficult to learn *per se* and many people have navigated the changes that occur when these propositions are applied and the social organization of the school changes. In other words, we have passed the point where creating collaborative, high-energy environments in schools can be regarded as a formidable enterprise. Rather, solid, methodical effort is needed along with confidence that personnel can adapt to the needed changes without undue stress.

PROPOSITIONS

The focus of this chapter is the collective energy of the school and how to ensure that all school faculties have a high degree of synergy and cohesiveness.

Active Formal Leadership Is Essential

The call for active instructional leadership (Goodlad, 1984) has been so consistent that it has virtually become a cliche, but what an important truism of practice it is (Leithwood & Montgomery, 1982; Fullan, 1982; Crandall et al., 1982). Probably the most astounding aspect of the current discussions about the important role of the formal leadership at the site level (the principal and assistant principals or deans) is the notion that there could be any resident in those roles who does not perceive leadership as the critical element in his or her work.

Leadership needs to be very active in bringing about cohesion in the faculty, involvement of community members, the development of study groups, and connecting the school to systemic initiatives. Specific duties include:

1. Organizing the faculty into study groups and coaching teams; meeting with those teams and facilitating their activities.
2. Organizing a staff-development/school-improvement council to coordinate activities, select priorities, and ensure facilitation of clinical and systemic components.
3. Arranging for time for the collaborative study of teaching and the implementation of curricular and instructional innovations.
4. Becoming knowledgeable about training and the options for school improvement. (See chapters four to seven.) Ensuring that the staff is knowledgeable.
5. Participating in training and the implementation of collective and systemic initiatives. Knowledgeability is the key here, for an in-depth understanding of innovations in curriculum and instruction is necessary to plan facilitation.

6. Continuously assessing the educational climate of the school, feeding information and perspective to the faculty for use in decision making about possible areas for study and improvement.

The specific details are less important than the commitment to the role as curricular and instructional leader. Imagine the following description of one principal in action.

Lauren is principal of a twenty-classroom school in a rural area. In addition to the twenty teachers who are assigned to classrooms, there is a full-time librarian and special education resource teacher. Lauren has organized the faculty into four study groups. Each group is responsible for exploring a particular teaching strategy and preparing themselves not only to use that strategy but to demonstrate it for the other groups. Lauren, together with one member of each study group and five parents elected by the parent community, constitute the school committee (see Joyce, Hersh, & McKibbin, 1983, for a detailed description of the "Responsible Parties" in the school improvement process). The committee is responsible for organizing parents and community members to examine the educational health of the school and suggesting ways of improving curriculum, instruction, and social climate. Instructional strategies (Joyce & Weil, 1986) are the focus for the current two-year period.

The faculty gathers once a week in a informal meeting in a social setting with refreshments. Study groups report on their progress and watch a videotape of one of the teachers using one of the new instructional strategies.

In addition, Lauren, the librarian, and the resource teacher each teach one period each day, taking over classes from the other teachers, freeing them so that the coaching partnerships can function effectively. Lauren also visits the classroom of one teacher each day, trying to identify areas of need that can become the focus of the weekly meetings. It is on those visits that she makes the tapes that provide some of the substance of those meetings. Also, she is preparing herself to think through what she believes should be the next focus for school improvement — more effective use of the computer as an instructional tool. She is already aware that only two of the faculty members have more than the most primitive understanding of the possibilities, let alone skill in using computers themselves. She is discussing options with a consultant from the state department. Lauren knows that resources are available to increase the numbers of computers in the school and she is determined to work out a feasible plan and ensure a good implementation. However, she is also concerned that the science curriculum is very weak and wonders if strengthening the science curriculum is a greater priority than the computer or if the two objectives can be combined. She already plans to build on the study of instructional models to strengthen the science program, but she wisely doesn't want to overload the faculty by asking them to deal with too many initiatives at once.

One of the keys to Lauren's achievements as an instructional leader is that she has no doubt at all that it is her chief responsibility. She believes that she has the responsibility for organizing the faculty and involving community members in the development of the healthiest social climate, curriculum, and instructional setting that she can. Although Lauren is integrative and gentle, she is quietly forceful — everyone is involved in the decision-making process, but steady improvement is central in every meeting. She does not tolerate complacency.

Faculty Cohesion Must Be Established with Clear Understanding of the Obligations for Collective Action

The relatively solitary norms of teaching need to be replaced with a sense of the obligation for collective action. One of the major obstacles to school improvement efforts is that teachers and administrators have perceived the instructional role primarily in terms of what one individual does with classes of students and there has been a much less clear picture of the role as a collaborative faculty member. *Specifically, the governance of staff development and school improvement efforts depends on an understanding that the faculty and administration can make decisions that are binding on the members of the group.* Continuing the example above, Lauren and the school committee suggested that instructional strategies become the emphasis for a couple of years and the faculty voted on that proposal and several others. About three-quarters of the members placed instructional strategies first. The remainder of the faculty understood that they were obligated by the majority decision with respect to the collective component of staff development. (They were, of course, free to pursue other interests as part of the individual-governed clinical component.)

One of the essential aspects of Lauren's leadership is helping the faculty understand the difference in the dynamics of decision making between the several components. For example, no one is obligated to become a member of an instructional cadre offering training to others. However, once a school-improvement focus has been selected or the district has made an initiative, then all the members of the group are obligated to participate.

It is not uncommon for districts and schools to sidestep the issue by attempting "lateral diffusion" strategies, whereby, even when a majority decision is made, it is understood that it will begin with volunteer participation and rely on the success of the initial effort to spread the innovation. That strategy simply does not work in the social system of faculties as presently constituted (Joyce & Hersh, 1983). Also, a school-wide effort in curriculum, technology, or school climate requires collaboration if it is to work. To confine it to a group of volunteers is to deny the role of collective activity in implementation.

The Relationship between the School and the District Office Personnel Needs to Emphasize School Improvement in a Focused Manner

The central office personnel and school leadership have to be closely connected to build shared understandings about the importance of staff development and to ensure that it is focused properly. A district council needs to select the areas that will receive systemic initiative during any given period and these areas must be few and solidly backed. District office personnel need to be well-coordinated so that the school is not deluged by initiatives made by departments that end up competing for the time of teachers. In one district that we studied (Joyce, Bush, & McKibbin, 1982) a single school actually received more than 40 initiatives from the district office in one year. How can this happen, one might ask? The answer is because the zeal of the central office personnel was not accompanied by the tempering effects of coordination. Reading specialists were initiating a drive to improve the reading curriculum and offering workshops to primary teachers. Supervisors were initiating training in the ITIP mode as well as offering workshops to principals and administrators (Hunter,1980;1981). Special education supervisors were offering workshops on the integration of students with learning disabilities in the classroom. A new program in education for the "gifted and talented" was initiated. A new shipment of microcomputers arrived and was distributed along with a round of workshops on how to use them. We could go on and on.

The effect of this kind of "shotgun" from the central office is to trivialize all of the initiatives. With only a few persons receiving relatively weak training in any one of them, the entire range of efforts simply evaporates in a short period of time.

Such a diffused message simply confuses the schools that are disposed to cooperate and fuels the cynicism of those who are less disposed. The alternative is clear; the district staff development council needs to screen initiatives and select only one or two for a major effort. These systemic initiatives need to be communicated through the school representatives on the council to the school faculties, and preparations made to cooperate with the initiative. School councils need to take the system initiative into account as they establish the collective initiatives, pyramiding energy wherever possible. The study groups and coaching teams, of course, will be essential to both.

The district personnel also need to help administrators get the training and support they need to fulfill their roles effectively, providing training in content options for school-based initiatives and in the skills needed to organize councils, study groups, coaching teams, and training.

A spirit of cooperation is essential. Principals and teacher members of the district council need to approach the decision-making tasks to build cooperative relationships. They simply *must* understand that the clinical and collective components provide ample room for individual and school initiatives and *not* view the systemic component as an objectionable "lay-on" simply because it requires decision making and implementation for the entire district organization.

Active leadership from the superintendent is another priority. Richard Wallace, the superintendent in Pittsburgh, demonstrated the importance of the superintendent, even in a large system, during the organization of the Schenley program in Pittsburgh. Named for a school that became a staff-development center, the program has been organized so that in the three-year period beginning in the fall of 1983, *all* of the secondary teachers in the Pittsburgh school district spent two consecutive months, during one of the school years, in residence at Schenley. The school was restaffed with outstanding teachers drawn from all over the district and the visiting teachers worked with the resident staff and with a staff development team that conducted workshops on the analysis of teaching. A cadre of supernumerary teachers released the faculty members so that they could attend the Schenley program. The members of that cadre rotated from school to school, relieving teachers and providing program continuity (Wallace et al., 1984). Such a program could not be thought out, maintained, or implemented without a superintendent who is a highly visible and active instructional leader for the entire district. Administrators, teachers, teachers organizations, the school board, and the community at large have to develop and maintain a shared understanding powerful enough to sustain the substantial innovations in relationships necessary to carry out a strong staff development program.

Returning to Lauren, her relationship with her district office sustains her activities. Although she is in a rural setting where it is difficult to have the regular contact that is easy to arrange in a more densely populated area, her superintendent and the rest of the central office staff have no doubt that her primary role is as instructional leader of her school. They do not deluge her with initiatives but maintain a council where she and a faculty representative meet periodically with their opposite numbers to define the systemic initiatives and divide resources. For example, the district has provided consultant services to her staff to maintain the program on instructional strategies. Reciprocally, she prepares her staff to cooperate with those systemic initiatives that are selected. She and the central office staff are well aware that curricular change has been extremely difficult in many districts (Fullan & Pomfret, 1977) and that substantial training and hard work in each school is necessary to implement any initiative of worth (Hall, 1986; Hall & Loucks, 1977).

Vertical and Horizontal Solidarity within a District is Essential if Planned Change is to Occur

The research on organizational development (Fullan & Park, 1981; Schmuck, Runkel, Arends, & Arends, 1977; Crandall et al., 1982) indicates clearly how important social cohesion is to the innovative process, and we stress again that many features and most of the worthy content of staff development are innovations in themselves.

It is only because of the isolation that has characterized teaching that so much attention needs to be given to the development of cohesion. Teachers have been separated from one another in the workplace and, further, have been separated from administrators in the loosely coupled organization of the school and school districts (Baldridge & Deal, 1975). If education professionals had been in closer contact with one another, the development of social cohesion would not require so much attention at this time.

Labor relations have become an important part of the process of building collective action, and collective bargaining is going to be an increasingly important feature of the educational scene. We find the emphasis put on staff development by some of the recent organization publications and activities to be very important (Rauth et al., 1983). The involvement in decision making is very important and the system we envision provides for it handsomely. Some of the bargaining items in recent years have less appeal. For example, in some districts organizations have bargained for fewer faculty meetings. This would enormously reduce the possibilities for collective action and will, if it continues, result in a loss of power by teachers, for it is only through meetings that power manifests itself in the daily process of operating the school and the school district. Similarly, there have been some cases where teachers' organizations have bargained to separate administrators from common training with them, which would prevent supervisors, administrators, and teachers from studying together and engaging in collective activity. Also, some organizations have opposed having teachers study one another's teaching on the ground that constitutes a quasi-supervisory activity and is confounded with evaluation.

It is better, we believe, when organizations bargain for greater amounts of staff development and for the conditions that promote cohesiveness and involvement in decision making. Many blue-collar workers have bargained to separate themselves from foremen and middle-management personnel, effectively reducing the day-to-day shared involvement that ultimately would keep them in the picture as the workplace has been shaped. They have relied on the power of formal bargaining, supported with strike threats, to enforce formal demands. Physicians, however, have bargained with hospitals and other organizations for professional involvement at virtually every level of management, thus keeping themselves in the picture as day-by-day decisions are made that affect practice and working conditions. Further, medical professionals would not think of bargaining to *reduce* either further training in content and skills, or for a lesser role in working with their peers to analyze and improve their practice.

Education professionals have to be careful to formulate bargaining procedures that make professional development a part of the responsibility of the organization and teacher involvement in decision making a collective process. Bargaining for greater isolation from peers and administrators (under the name of autonomy) is seductive, because it avoids the hard work of learning to collaborate and submit oneself to instruction, but ultimately it would be destructive.

Districts, for their part, have to be careful not to bargain away the opportunity for staff development and collective activity because it seems easier to concede in those areas rather than in salary and benefit programs.

SUMMARY

All of the propositions discussed above have as one of their major purposes to bring people together for collective decision making and action. Shared understanding about both content and process are necessary for collective action to occur. The development of study groups is symbolic of the need for cooperative action to implement the substance of staff development. The coaching partnerships are symbolic of the notion that teachers can learn from other teachers and share the process of learning new content and teaching methods. The existence of the councils is a statement that trust can be built to develop a place in which learning by teachers can be given an important place in the life of the school.

We hear much these days about the difficulties in the workplace (McLaughlin, 1986) and the dilemmas of leadership in a time when members of the teaching staff feel burned out and unsupported. The antidote is an active workplace that propels educators into collaborative, growth-producing activity. A strong, upbeat staff development program is a major part of the prescription.

CHAPTER FOUR

EDUCATIONAL ENVIRONMENTS AND STUDENT LEARNING: THE BOTTOM LINE OF STAFF DEVELOPMENT

It could be argued that the benefits to personnel and organization are by themselves a sufficient rationale for the development of a strong staff development system and that increased student learning might be something "nice if we can have it, too." However, in this chapter we will concentrate on the benefits that accrue directly to students from the study of teaching, curriculum, school improvement, and technology. We will argue that the student learning benefits are so great that the failure to create a strong staff development system is a tragic dereliction.

During the last twenty-five years there has been a great expansion of the number of research and development personnel in education and applied psychology, with a consequent enlargement of the output of educational research that can be applied to practice. Although there has been a great effort to make this information available to school personnel (Walberg, 1986), very little of it has been incorporated in staff development programs. At this time educational research provides an array of serious candidates for the substance of programs that would increase student learning.

In the pages that follow we present a selective review of some of the areas that show promise, with particular emphasis on the amounts and types of achievement that can be expected from a careful implementation of the results. A major purpose of the human resource development system is to ensure that all personnel are aware of the magnitude of effects that can be achieved when innovations are used properly. Whenever individual teachers, school faculties, or a school system engage in training, a major part of the commitment to participate and put the substance into operation should be based on an appreciation of the benefits that can accrue to students.

Given our position that the content for the individual, collective, and systemic components of the system should be supported by research or have a firm rationale behind them, we will begin with a discussion of the types of research that have been conducted on teaching, curriculum, effective schools, and the role of knowledge in teaching effectiveness. We will concentrate on identifying potential content for the components of the staff development system, including teaching practices, dimensions of effective schools, and curriculum. In chapter five we will propose a framework that can be used for selecting content for the system, using practices supported by research and other sources.

SOURCES OF PROMISING PRACTICES

The concept of validated educational practice defines one of the most promising areas for bringing educational research and practice together (Joyce, Showers, Dalton, & Beaton, 1985). If research can identify effective teaching skills and they can be incorporated as the objectives of preservice and inservice teacher education programs, the distance between the activities of scholars and practitioners can be greatly reduced (Gage, 1978; Medley, 1977). The yield from four distinct lines of inquiry has now accumulated to the point where we can assess the findings and begin to organize the results in a form that can be useful for program planning. The four lines of inquiry are

- Models of teaching—studies of theories of curriculum and instruction
- Studies of curriculum and curriculum implementation
- Studies of schools thought to be effective
- Studies of teachers thought to be effective

When these are considered together, the body of research is substantial. Each broadens the concept of educational practice by illuminating different aspects of the work of teachers.

THE CONCEPT OF EFFECT SIZE

We use a concept called "effect size" to describe the magnitude of gains from any given change in educational practice and thus to predict what we can hope to accomplish by using that practice.

To introduce the idea, let us consider a study conducted by Dr. Bharati Baveja with the authors in the Motilal Nehru School of Sports about thirty miles northwest of New Delhi, India. Dr. Baveja designed her study to test the effectiveness of an inductive approach to a botany unit against an intensive tutorial treatment. All of the students were given a test at the beginning of the unit to assess their knowledge before instruction began and were divided into two groups equated on the basis of achievement. The control group studied the material with the aid of tutoring and lectures on the material – the standard treatment in Indian schools for courses of this type. The experimental group worked in pairs and were led through inductive and concept attainment exercises emphasizing classification of plants.

Figure 2 shows the distribution of scores for the experimental and control groups on the posttest which, like the pretest, contained items dealing with the information pertaining to the unit.

The difference between the experimental and control groups was a little

Figure 2. Compared Distributions for Experimental and Control Groups: Baveja Study

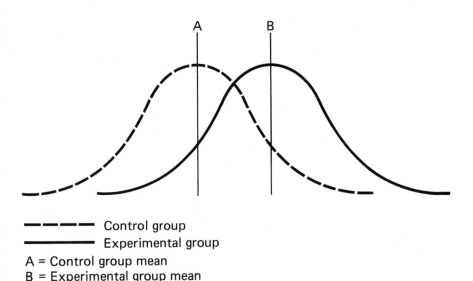

――――― Control group
――――― Experimental group
A = Control group mean
B = Experimental group mean

above a standard deviation. The difference, computed in terms of standard deviations, is the effect size of the inductive treatment. Essentially, what that means is that the experimental group average score (50th percentile) was where the 80th-percentile score was for the control group. The difference increased when a delayed recall test was given ten months later, indicating that the information acquired with the concept-oriented strategies was retained somewhat better than information gained via the control treatment.

Calculations like these enable us to compare the magnitude of the potential effects of the innovations (teaching skills and strategies, curriculums, and technologies) that we might use in an effort to affect student learning. We can also determine whether the treatment has different effects for all kinds of students or just for some. In the study just described, the experimental treatment was apparently effective for the whole population. The lowest score in the experimental group distribution was about where the 30th-percentile score was for the control group, and about 30 percent of the students exceeded the highest score obtained in the control.

Although substantial in its own right, learning and retention of information was modest when we consider the effect on the students' ability to identify plants and their characteristics, which was measured on a separate test. The scores by students from the experimental group were *eight* times higher than the scores for the control group. The inference is that the inductive treatment enabled students to apply the information and concepts from the unit much more effectively than the students from the tutorial treatment were able to.

Although high effect sizes make a treatment attractive, size alone is not the only consideration when choosing among alternatives. Modest effect sizes that affect many persons can have a large payoff for the population. A comparison with medicine is worthwhile. Suppose a dread disease is affecting a population and we possess a vaccine that will reduce the chances of contracting the disease by only 10 percent. If a million persons might become infected without the vaccine but only 900,000 if it is used, the modest effect of the vaccine might save 100,000 lives. In education, some estimates suggest that during the first year of school about one million children each year (about 30 percent) make little progress toward learning to read. We also know that lack of success in reading instruction is in fact a dread educational disease, since for each year that initial instruction is unsuccessful the probability that the student will respond to instruction later is greatly lowered. Would a modestly effective treatment, say one that reduced the lack of success in the first year for 50,000 children (five percent) be worthwhile? We think so. Also, several such treatments might cumulate. Of course, we prefer a high-effect treatment, but one is not always available. Even when it is, it might not reach some students and we might need to resort to a less powerful choice for those students.

Also, there are different types of effects that need to be considered. Attitudes, values, concepts, intellectual development, skills, and information are just a few. Keeping to the example of early reading, two treatments might be approximately equal in terms of learning to read in the short run, but one might affect attitudes positively and leave the students feeling confident and ready to try again. Similarly, two social studies programs might achieve the learning of similar amounts of information and concepts, but one might excel in teaching attitudes toward citizenship.

Throughout the remainder of the book we will refer to the sizes of effects obtained in studies of educational practices in three categories:

- *Modestly effective.* These are practices that increase learning of particular kinds by up to one-half of a standard deviation. Compared to standard treatments, these increase the learning of the average students to between the 60th and 70th percentile of a control group in an experimental study.
- *Substantially effective.* These practices can increase student learning from one-half to one standard deviation. The average student, when these treatments are used, falls between the 70th and 80th percentile when compared to a control group receiving standard instruction.
- *Very effective.* These practices can increase learning more than one standard deviation. In the most dramatic instances, when the effect size reaches five or six standard deviations, the lowest-scoring student in the experimental treatment exceeds the highest-scoring student in the control treatment! This is a rare event, of course, but when it does occur, it gives us great hope about the potential of educational practice.

Again, as we describe some practices and the effects that can be expected from them, we should not concentrate on magnitude of effects alone. Self-instructional programs that are no more effective than standard instruction can be very useful because they enable students to teach themselves and can be blended with agent-delivered instruction. Broadcast television, because of its potential to reach so many children, can make a big difference even though it is modestly effective in comparison with standard instruction. "Sesame Street" and "The Electric Company" are examples. They are not dramatically more effective than first-grade instruction in reading, but they produce positive attitudes and augment instruction handsomely, enabling a certain percentage of students to virtually teach themselves to read (Ball & Bogatz, 1970).

MODELS OF TEACHING

From psychology, social psychology, philosophy, therapy and other disciplines have come experiments designed to learn whether theoretically derived patterns of teaching produce the distinctive effects for which they were designed (Joyce & Weil, 1986). Most models of teaching are designed for specific purposes—the teaching of information, concepts, ways of thinking, the study of social values, and so forth by asking students to engage in cognitive and social tasks that are unlikely to occur in many classrooms. The testing of these teaching models generally begins with a thesis describing an educational environment, its presumed effects, and a rationale that links the environment and its intended effects—how to develop concepts or to learn them, how to build theories, memorize information, solve problems, learn skills. Some center on delivery by the instructor, while others develop as the learners respond to tasks and the student is regarded as a partner in the educational enterprise (Joyce & Weil, 1986). Testing instructional models requires training teachers to use them. The first step in theory-driven research is often the collection of baseline data about how the teachers normally teach. Then, the teachers are trained to use the new teaching behaviors. Implementation of the new behavior is monitored, either in the regular classroom or in a laboratory setting, and theory-relevant student behaviors or outcomes are measured. Experimental classrooms are often compared with traditional classrooms to determine the presence, direction, and magnitude of change. In a very few studies, combinations of theories have been intensively employed to attempt to influence intelligence and personality (Spaulding, 1970). Since nearly all teachers use "recitation" or "lecture-recitation" as the primary mode of teaching (Goodlad, 1984; Goodlad & Klein, 1970; Hoetker & Ahlbrand, 1969; Sirotnik, 1983), training in new strategies must often be intensive.

Some researchers have studied teaching skills that they believe can affect achievement when quite a number of teaching strategies are being used. Examples that we will discuss later include "wait time" (Tobin, 1986) and creating an affirmative classroom climate (Kerman, 1979). The research strategy is similar—teaching teachers how to use the skill and observing the effects on teacher behavior and achievement. Researchers then determine how well the skills can be taught to practitioners and whether the effects approximate those in the controlled tests. Single models have in some cases been studied several hundred times. The effort involved in examining them is rewarding. The practices are complex and powerful. In most cases the intellective component of the teaching skills is fairly substantial: The teacher needs to master the theory of the model and learn to apply it to academic substance and instructional materials. It is also necessary to create the social system appropriate to the model, induce the students to engage in the cognitive and social tasks of the model, and modulate those according to the responses of the students. In nearly all cases the mastery of a model by the students is the key to effectiveness – the students have to learn how to engage in the particular learning process emphasized by that model. We will concentrate on a few quite different models as illustrations, following the framework proposed by Joyce and Weil (1986) that classifies models according to the most prominent kinds of learning strategies they emphasize: personal, social, information-processing, or behavioral systems. In some cases researchers have concentrated on specific, "model-relevant" outcomes, whereas in other cases a broad spectrum of school outcomes have been examined.

The Effects of Selected Social Models of Teaching

There have been three lines of research on ways of helping students study and learn together. Currently these are most popularly known as "cooperative learning" approaches to teaching. One is that of David and Roger Johnson and their colleagues (1981), who have studied the effects of cooperative task and reward structures on learning. The Johnsons' (1975; 1981) work on peers-teaching-peers has provided us with information about the effects of cooperative behavior on both traditional learning tasks and on values and intergroup behavior and attitudes. Slavin's extensive review (1983) includes the study of a variety of approaches where he manipulates the complexity of the social tasks and experiments with various types of groupings. Slavin reported success with heterogeneous groups on tasks requiring coordination of group members on both academic learning and intergroup relations. Group Investigation is the most complex of the social models of teaching. It begins with a confrontation with a puzzling situation. The students react to the situation and examine the nature of their common and different reactions. They determine what kinds of information they need to approach the problem and proceed to collect relevant data. They generate hypotheses and gather the information needed to test them. They evaluate their products and continue their inquiry or begin a new line of inquiry (Thelen, 1960; Sharan & Hertz-Lazarowitz, 1980). The teaching skills are those that build the cooperative social environment and teach students the skills of negotiation and conflict resolution necessary for democratic problem solving. In addition, the teacher needs to guide the students in methods of data collection and analysis, help them frame testable hypotheses, and decide what would constitute a reasonable test of a hypothesis. Because groups vary considerably in their need for structure (Hunt, 1971) and their cohesiveness (Thelen, 1967), the teacher cannot behave mechanically but must "read" the students' social and academic behavior and provide the assistance that keeps the inquiry moving without squelching it. The research that underlies the model consists partly of tests of the general thesis of the social family – that cooperative activity generates synergistic energy that advances learning – and partly directly tests the model itself – that group investigation builds democratic-process skills, increases social cohesion, and results in the learning of information, concepts, and the processes of academic inquiry. Sharan and his associates (1982) studied the effects of different degrees of implementation. Results showed the stronger the implementation, the greater the effects on both lower-order and higher-order academic learning, with the largest effects, as predicted, on higher-order outcomes. The children also learned the skills required by the model and group cohesion and intergroup attitudes were affected positively. Sharan and his associates, through their careful study of implementation, documented the need for extensive training and for the formation of a community of teachers who could help one another perfect their use of this complex model. (See chapters six, seven, and eight.)

What is the magnitude of effects that we can expect when teachers learn to use the cooperative learning strategies effectively? In Rolheiser-Bennett's (1986) review she compared the effects of the degrees of cooperative structure required by the several approaches, the group investigation model being the most extreme.

For the highly structured systems of teaching students to study together, she found that the average effect size on standardized tests in the basic curriculum areas (such as reading and mathematics) was 0.28 with some studies approaching half a standard deviation. On criterion-referenced tests the average was 0.48 with some of the best implementations reaching an effect of about one standard deviation.

The somewhat more elaborate cooperative learning models had an average effect size of somewhat more than one standard deviation, with some exceeding two standard deviations. (The average student was above the 90th percentile student in the control group.) The effects on higher-order thinking were even greater, with an average effect of about 1.25 standard deviations and effects in some studies as high as 3.0 standard deviations. Taken as a whole, research on cooperative learning is overwhelmingly positive – nearly every study has had from modest to very high effects. Moreover, the cooperative approaches are effective over a range of achievement measures. The more intensely cooperative the environment, the greater the effects, and the more complex the outcomes (higher-order processing of information, problem solving), the greater the effects.

The cooperative environment engendered by these models has had substantial effects on the cooperative behavior of the students, increasing feelings of empathy for others, reducing intergroup tensions and aggressive and antisocial behavior, improving moral judgment, and building positive feelings toward others, including those of other ethnic groups. Many of these effect sizes are substantial — one or two standard deviations is not uncommon and one is as high as eight.

What does this mean for the skills to implement cooperative learning models as an outcome of staff development? Clearly, we believe, the cooperative learning skills are viable candidates for intensive staff development. As we will see, they are not the only candidates.

Effects from Selected Information-Processing Models

There are quite a number of models of teaching that are designed to increase students' ability to process information more powerfully. These include methods for presenting information so that students can learn and retain it more effectively by operating on it more conceptually, systems that assist memorization and teach students how to organize information for mastery, models to teach students to collect and organize information conceptually (such as the ones previously described in the study of inductive thinking), and ones to teach students to use the methods of the disciplines, to engage in causal reasoning, and to master concepts (Joyce & Weil, 1986).

Many of these models have an extensive recent research literature (the number for each approach ranges from about a dozen to more than 300). We will discuss just two here, advance organizers and approaches to mnemonics, although research relevant to the disciplines-oriented inductive approach will be included in the discussion of the effects of curriculums, below.

Advance Organizers

David Ausubel's formulation (1963) that there would be greater retention of materials from presentations and reading if the material was accompanied by organizing ideas has generated more than two hundred studies. Essentially, lectures, assignments of reading and research, and courses are accompanied by presentations of concepts that help the student increase intellectual activity during and after exposure to information. The early studies involved much experimentation with ways of formulating and delivering organizers. Because of modest findings some reviewers asserted that the line of endeavor was not productive (Barnes and Clausen, 1975). The technique advanced quite a bit during the 1970s, however, and current reviewers are quite positive (Lawton and Wanska, 1977; Luiten, Ames, and Ackerson, 1980). Rolheiser-Bennett's (1986) review of eighteen recent investigations turned up an average effect size of lower-order achievement (such as the recall of information and concepts) of 1.35. (With such an effect the average student studying with the aid of organizers learned about as much as the 90th percentile student studying the same material without the assistance of the organizing ideas.) The effects on higher-order thinking (transfer of concepts to new material, etc.) averaged 0.42. Longer-term studies obtained somewhat better results than did short-term studies, presumably because the organizing ideas became better anchored in the minds of the students and had greater facilitating effect.

Stone's (1983) analysis indicated that organizers are effective across ages, being somewhat more effective for students at the stage of concrete operations, when students may need more assistance formulating abstract ideas to anchor content, and across curriculum areas. Illustrations add to the effectiveness of organizers and the impact is increased when they lead to activities and generalizations. While they affect several kinds of outcomes, recall of facts and formulas are most affected. The prediction that can be made is that teachers who accompany presentations and written assignments with organizers will have consistent, although sometimes modest, effects on the learning of information and concepts. Because readings and lectures repeatedly reach so many learners, the cumulative potential is great. Also, structuring a course around organizers, organizing presentations and assignments within the course, tying the organizers to activities that require their application, and illustrating them, can have effects as high as two standard deviations. (With an effect of that size the lowest achieving students are about where the average student would be when studying without the help of organizers. The rest of the distribution is comparably above the control.)

The primary skills required by teachers if they are to use organizers are cognitive in nature. To frame organizers one needs to study the material the students are to study and generate ideas that can provide for the learner what Ausubel calls an "intellectual scaffolding" that can hold the information and concepts to be learned. The formulation of the organizers is difficult, as indicated by the modest results in much of the early research, but recently much-improved guidelines have emerged. The presentation of organizers is not difficult, and the time to prepare illustrations with appropriate media appears to pay off substantially. Clearly the advance organizer technology is a candidate for staff development activities.

Mnemonics (Systems to Improve Memorization)

Although research on memorization and mnemonic strategies has been conducted for more than one hundred years, until a few years ago most of the yield for school practice offered few and very general guidelines, such as advice about when to mass and when to distribute practice. Little research had been conducted on the learning of school subjects. In the mid-1970s a productive line of work was begun by Atkinson at Stanford University which has been greatly extended by Pressley and Levin at the Universities of Western Ontario and Wisconsin. They have developed a series of systems for organizing information to promote memory and have given particular, although not exclusive attention to one known as the "link-word" method. Atkinson applied the method during experiments with computer-assisted instruction in which he was attempting to increase students' learning of initial foreign-language vocabularies. He experimented with what he called "acoustic" and "imagery" links. The first was designed to make associations between foreign pronunciations and the sounds of known English words. The second was used to make the connection vivid (Atkinson, 1975). In one early study the link method produced as much learning in two trials as the conventional method did in three. The experimental group learned about half as many words more than the control group and maintained the advantage after several weeks. He also found that the method was enhanced when the students supplied their own imagery.

Further developmental work included experiments with children of various ages and across subjects. Using a link-word system in Spanish vocabulary learning, second and fifth grade children learned about twice the words as did children using rote and rehearsal methods (Pressley, 1977). In later work with Levin and Miller (1981), Pressley employed a "pictured action" variant of the method with first and sixth grade children, who acquired three times as much vocabulary as did control groups. With Dennis-Rounds (1980) he extended the strategy to social studies information (products and cities) and learned that students could transfer the method to other learning tasks with instruction. Pressley, Levin, and McCormick (1980) found that primary school students could generate sentences to enhance memorization. The results were three times as great as for students using their own methods. Similar results were found with kindergarten and preschool children (Pressley et al., 1981). With Levin and Miller (1981) the work was successfully extended to vocabulary with abstract meanings. Levin and his colleagues (1983) have also extended the application to abstract prose.

It was important to learn whether better "natural" memorizers, with practice, develop their own equivalent methods. Pressley, Levin, and Ghatala (1984) asked whether students, with age and practice, would spontaneously develop elaborated methods for memorizing material and found that very few did. The better performers had, however, developed more elaborate methods than the majority, who used rote-rehearsal methods alone. However, the newly developed mnemonic methods enhanced learning across the range. Hence, it appears that the method or an equivalent one can be very beneficial for most students. The consistency of the findings is impressive. The link-word method appears to have general applicability across subject matters and ages of children (Pressley, Levin, & Delaney, 1982) and can be used by teachers and taught to children.

The effect sizes reached by many of the studies are quite high. The *average* for transfer tasks (where the material learned was to be applied in another setting), was 1.91. Recall of attributes of items (such as towns, cities, minerals) was 1.5. Foreign-language acquisition was 1.3, with many studies reporting very high outcomes. Delayed recall generally maintained the gains, indicating that the mnemonics strategies have a lasting effect.

The teaching skills required to use these methods with students are largely cognitive. Generating the links is the chief activity. Once they have been generated and the materials prepared, the presentation to the students is easily done, whether through work sheets, computer, media, or presentation by the teacher. The results on transfer of the method to other tasks is particularly important. A possible application is for all teachers and students to study how to memorize and to learn how to use mnemonics generally in teaching and learning activities. The study of metacognitive processes, whereby students become more aware of the processes of learning and guide their behavior accordingly, has important implications for the conduct of education in general.

Other Information-Processing Models

The massive data base underlying the many alternative models of teaching prevents us from providing even brief reviews of the entire spectrum. However, we need to deal lightly with a number of them, especially ones designed to teach thinking skills, the size of the knowledge base under many models of teaching prevents us from providing even brief reviews of the entire spectrum. However, we need to deal lightly with a number of them, especially ones designed to teach thinking skills, due to the substantial interest in them at this time (Costa, 1985; Marzano et al., 1987; Perkins, 1986; Sternberg, 1986).

Models taken directly from the sciences have been the basis for curriculums for both elementary and high school children. A description of the teaching skills and the effects of the science-based curriculums is included in a later section of this book. The results of the research indicate that the scientific method can be taught and has positive effects on the acquisition of information, concepts, and attitudes. More narrowly defined studies have been made on inductive teaching and inquiry training. Beginning with Taba's (1966) exploration of an inductive social studies curriculum, periodic small-scale studies have probed the area. In 1968 Worthen provided evidence to support one of its central theses – that induced concepts would facilitate long-term recall. Feeley (1972) reviewed the social science studies and reported that differences in terminology hampered the accumulation of research but that the inductive methods generally lived up to expectations, generating concept development and positive attitudes.   Research on Suchman's (1964) model for teaching causal reasoning directly supported the proposition that inquiry training can be employed with both elementary and high school children. Schrenker (1976) reported that inquiry training resulted in increased understanding of science, greater productivity in critical thinking, and skills for obtaining and analyzing information.   He reported that it made little difference in the mastery of information, per se, but that it was as efficient as didactic methods or the didactic cum laboratory methods generally employed to teach science.   Ivany (1969) and Collins (1969) examined variants in the kinds of confrontations and materials used and reported that the strength of the confrontation as a stimulus to inquiry was important and that richness in instructional materials was a significant factor.   Elefant (1980) successfully carried out the strategy with deaf children in an intriguing study that has implications for work with all children.   Voss' (1982) general review includes an annotation of a variety of studies that are generally supportive of the approach.

The skills of these models apparently require intensive training.   Teachers need to study the substance of a lesson, unit, or curriculum and develop a rich array of instructional materials that can be explored by the children.   They have to guide concept - formation activities and help the students become more sophisticated in the making of categories and inferences.   The flow of instruction emerges, depending on the thinking of the students, and the environment has to be adjusted to the developing lesson.   Knowledge of both the substance and process appear to be critical.

Reviews (Sternberg, 1986; Sternberg & Bahna, 1986) of some of the recently developed packages for teaching elements of analytic reasoning to students have reported modest effects for some of them.

For staff-development policy, an important implication of the research on the inductive and inquiry-oriented models of teaching is that the processes of inductive and analytic reasoning can be taught effectively to students in the context of curriculums in the basic school subjects.   To do so on a wide scale requires that teachers learn the substance and the teaching technologies that will enable them to design and implement lessons, units, and courses around these models.

Personal Models of Teaching

Student-centered models are numerous and controversial.   From a scientific point of view it is unfortunate that the literature is so rhetorical and that so many personalists have devoted energy to diatribes against traditional methods or even against the work of theorists of other persuasions. Only in the last ten years has considerable energy been devoted to research to explore the dynamics of these methods in school settings and to deal directly with the serious concern of their critics – that person-centered education may neglect the development of academic outcomes.

An interesting exception is the work with synectics (Gordon & Poze, 1971), which is designed both to enhance personal flexibility and creativity and to teach another of the higher-order thinking skills, specifically the ability to think divergently and generate alternative and relevant solutions to difficult problems and alternative perspectives on important concepts and values.

Research on synectics indicates that it achieves its "model-relevant" purposes, increasing student generation of ideas, divergent solutions to problems, and fluency in expressing ideas. (Effect sizes average 1.5 for generation of ideas and problem solving.) By helping students develop more multidimensional perspectives, it also increases recall of material from written passages by an effect size of 2.0 and the information is retained at an even higher level.

For policy in most school districts, what will be of most interest is that teaching students to think creatively is positively related with the learning and retention of information and can increase the lower-order outcomes to a substantial degree.

Nondirective Teaching.

Carl Rogers' *Freedom to Learn in the Eighties* (1982) includes a chapter summarizing much of the research from the humanistic perspective. Aspy (1969) and Roebuck, Buhler, and Aspy (1976) have been very productive over the last fifteen years. They have explored several of the theses of the family of personal models, particularly that building self-directed, empathetic communities of learners, will have positive effects on students' feelings about themselves and others and, consequently, will free energy for learning. Roebuck, Buhler, and Aspy's (1976) study with students identified as having learning difficulties produced positive effects on self-concept, interroup attitudes and interaction patterns, achievement in reading and mathematics, and increased scores on tests of intelligence. In studies of classroom teachers, they have documented the need for extensive training (Aspy, et al., 1974). The students of teachers who had learned the model thoroughly achieved more, felt better about themselves, had better attendance records, and improved their interpersonal skills. The model of nondirective teaching is very complex. Teachers have to develop egalitarian relationships with the students, create a cooperative group of students who respect one another's differences in personality and ability, help those students develop programs of study (including goals and the means for achieving them), provide feedback about performance and behavior and teach the students to reflect on one another's behavior and performance, help individuals and groups evaluate progress, and maintain an affirmative social climate. We think that the research personnel from the personalistic school of thought have answered their critics, and have developed a teachable technology. That technology requires a thorough knowledge of the theory of the approach and how to use it in the development of the educational environment. Because more than ordinary behaviors are necessary to implement the personalistic models, extensive training and practice are required.

Behavioral Systems Models

This family, based on the work of B. F. Skinner and the cybernetic training psychologists (Smith & Smith, 1966) has the largest literature. Studies range from programmed instruction to simulations and include training models (Joyce & Showers, 1983) and methods derived directly from therapy (Wolpe & Lazarus, 1966). There is a great deal of research on the application of social learning theory to instruction (Becker & Gersten, 1982), training (Smith & Smith, 1966), and simulations (Boocock & Schild, 1968). The behavioral technologists have demonstrated that they can design programs for both specific and general goals (Becker & Gersten, 1982) and also that the effective application of those techniques requires extensive cognitive activity and precise interactive skills (Spaulding, 1970).

A recent analysis by White (1986) examined the results of studies on the application of the DISTAR version of social learning theory to special education. The average effect sizes for mathematics and reading ranged from about one-half to one standard deviation. The effects for moderately and severely handicapped students were similar. Perhaps most important are a few studies in which the effects on aptitude (measures of intellectual ability) were included and where the DISTAR program was implemented for several years, the effect sizes were 1.0 or above, representing an increase of about 10 points in the standard IQ ratio.

Summary of Research on Teaching Models

Have the developers of theory proven that they can design effective approaches to teaching? We think they have. With modification, most of them have applicability across subject and grade lines, although some of them have been developed for particular subjects or ages. For example, the Jurisprudential model was created specifically to prepare secondary school students to analyze public policy questions. Does the application of the theory-driven models endanger the traditional goals of the school? By no means. On the contrary, they enhance the traditional goals of the school. What is the nature of the teaching skills necessary for use of these models? We think that the cognitive and interactive aspects are intertwined. Effective implementation of each requires a thorough understanding of the theory and the means to provide to students cognitive and social tasks that are presently unusual in the classroom.

Specific Teaching Practices Applicable Across Models and Styles

A number of research and development teams have developed ideas about aspects of the instructional act that reasonably might facilitate student achievement and feelings of self-worth if they are used regularly, regardless of the model of instruction that is used or the stylistic preferences of the instructors. We will deal with just two of these here: first, the concept of "wait-time," because of its long research history and second, Teacher Expectations and Student Achievement (TESA), because its wide dissemination in workshops sponsored by the Phi Delta Kappa organization has made it one of the most-used offerings in staff development programs across the country.

The concept of wait-time was formulated by Rowe (1969, 1974), who has long had a concern with the relationship between instructor behavior and the intellectual and affective engagement by the students. On first encountering the concept, it seems simple and uncomplicated enough. Rowe had observed, as had other students of teaching, that many classrooms are characterized by brief statements or questions by teachers and students that are densely packed into the time period. (In one study by the present authors there were as many as 250 utterances between teacher and students in an average *hour* of instruction—the average communication lasting only about two seconds!) She theorized that such a density fragments thought processes, not allowing students enough time to process the information contained in one communication before another is upon them. The teacher, controlling the interaction in a staccato fashion, also left the students cognitively and socially powerless—if a student thought for a few seconds and had something important to say, the time would have passed, with the discourse several communications down the road. Rowe speculated that if instructors slowed down the pace by *waiting more between communications,* then the students would be enabled to think over what was being discussed, would have more to say, would become more involved, and would be empowered to bring their cognitions into the discourse to a higher degree. Also, they would be more inclined to listen to one another and to comment on one another's ideas. In other words, she expected that the practice of waiting between communications would affect many other aspects of classroom interaction.

A recent study by Tobin (1986) lends the best support thus far to Rowe's theory. He successfully trained teachers to teach units in mathematics and language arts lessons and found a number of interesting effects. Among these were that the students were more often able to respond to questions (presumably because they had time to think about them and formulate their responses), their utterances became longer, and they were more likely to respond to one another. The teachers became more positive, and in language arts asked more questions that dealt with comprehension rather than simple recall of what had been read. The differences were actually manifested in student achievement with a modest effect size (about 0.2). That the effect is modest should not disqualify it from being considered as a candidate for a staff development program. The practice is clear and easy to understand, teachers can acquire the requisite behaviors quickly, and they are appropriate for many situations. A modest behavioral change that improves the quality of classroom discourse and is likely to increase student involvement and pay off regularly in achievement-related terms is, from our perspective, a fine candidate for our attempts to improve our teaching.

Kerman (1979) and his associates developed the Teacher Expectations and Student Achievement program from their observation that students in the same classroom are often treated differently, frequently without the teacher being aware of the differences, in ways that can affect their engagement and achievement. Specifically, the students with poorer learning histories are often called on less, giving them less opportunity for involvement, and often their responses are treated more negatively. Gradually the students become less involved and feel less valued. In discussions with teachers Kerman found that many had rational explanations for the differential treatment, citing a desire not to embarrass the low achievers and also to allow the higher achievers to talk more to bring out better and more correct ideas. Hence, procedures were developed to help teachers, through observation and feedback, to get a picture of the distribution and nature of the communications in their classroom and provide them with ideas about how to involve all the students affirmatively. A large body of research on teaching was used as sources of ideas for helping students respond, treating varieties of responses, maintaining a high level of respect and courtesy in the classroom, and so on. Their training has been successful and their formal studies indicate that the increased involvement by all students has an effect on student learning of about the same magnitude as wait-time. Again, they have provided a very direct avenue to helping teachers produce what most observers would agree is a more desirable classroom climate, an avenue that can be followed with modest amounts of training and that promises general educational benefits in the personal, social, and academic domains.

When we discuss the results of the naturalistic studies of teaching, below, we will discuss some other practices that have promise for improving instruction.

CURRICULUM STUDIES

Initiatives to improve curriculum areas or to establish new ones are especially important to the systemic and collective components of the staff development system. It has been well established that curriculum implementation is demanding of staff development — essentially, without strong staff development programs that are appropriately designed a very low level of implementation occurs (Fullan & Pomfret, 1977; Fullan, 1982).

The curriculum of schools — what is taught and how it is taught — obviously affects what students learn as a product of their engagement in schooling. Over the years much of the content that students are exposed to in the common curriculum areas has been relatively standardized. Nearly everyone can describe the content of elementary school arithmetic courses, for example, and almost any high school science teacher has a fairly good idea of the major topics that are likely to be covered in physics courses or advanced-placement chemistry courses. Yet there are differences between schools and school districts. In elementary school language arts programs, for example, the amount of attention to writing and literature differs quite a bit. In science the amount of time devoted to laboratory work varies.

Over the years variants on the standard courses have developed so that it is possible for quite a variety to be used, both with respect to content and teaching process. The important question to be dealt with here is how much difference there is when different materials, teaching processes, and content are implemented. We stress *implemented,* because a different plan will not by itself give us differences. In a sense, the fundamental question is whether we possess a technology that offers the prospect of more powerful curriculums so that districts have serious choices both in what is selected and in whether they will devote the staff development energy to implementing the curriculums they choose. A second important question is whether faculties can learn to use them. A third is whether conditions can be developed in schools to stabilize the curriculums so that they can have effects.

If the answers to these questions are affirmative, then teaching skills derived from formulations of curriculum can legitimately be employed as the objectives of teacher education.

Currently the clearest evidence about the potential effects on students comes from the study of the academically oriented curriculums in science and mathematics that were developed and used during the twenty-year period from 1955 to 1975 and from the experience with elementary curriculums in a variety of subject areas (Becker & Gersten, 1982; Rhine, 1981). The theory of the academic curriculums was relatively straightforward. The essence of the position was stated in *The Process of Education* (Bruner, 1961) and Schwab and Brandwein's *The Teaching of Science* (1962). The teaching of science should be as much as possible a simulation of the scientific process itself. The concepts of the disciplines should be studied rigorously in relation to their knowledge base. Thus science would be learned as inquiry. Further, the information thus learned would be retained well because it would be embedded in a meaningful framework and the student would possess the interrelated concepts that make up the structure of the disciplines.

In the academic reform movement of the 1950s and 1960s, entire curriculums in the sciences (e.g., BSCS Biology), social studies (e.g., Man, A Course of Study), mathematics (e.g., School Mathematics Study Group), and language (e.g., the linguistic approaches) were developed and introduced into the schools. These curriculums had in common their designers' beliefs that academic subjects should be studied with the tools of their respective disciplines. Most of these curriculums therefore required that students learn the modes of inquiry employed by the disciplines as well as factual material. Process was valued equally with content and many of these curriculums became characterized as "inquiry oriented." In addition, general approaches to early-childhood education (e.g., Headstart and Follow Through) and the education of older children (Individually Prescribed Instruction and DISTAR), studies of curriculums mediated through television and other media, and computer mediated and assisted curriculums make their contribution, even though some of them investigate the role of the human training agent in settings other than the classroom.

Much curriculum research resembles the experimental studies of teaching, but the unit under study is a configuration of content, teaching methods, instructional materials and technologies, and organizational forms. In the experiments any one of the elements of curriculum may be studied separately or in combination with the others, and the yield is expressed in terms of whether a curriculum produces predicted effects. Research on curriculum depends heavily on training in the content of the curriculum and the teaching strategies needed to implement it. Following training, implementation is monitored, either by classroom observation or interviews. Effects are determined by comparing student outcomes in experimental and control classrooms. In a few studies (e.g., Almy, 1970) combinations of curriculums are employed to determine effects on cognitive development and intelligence.

In both the academic reform movement and the early-childhood programs, elaborate curriculum materials were prepared to support the teaching/learning activities. The evaluation of the curriculums was difficult once it was learned that implementation was more arduous than had initially been thought. Only partial implementation occurred in many settings (Fullan & Pomfret, 1977). In the early stages research was meager and evaluation was poorly funded. However, eventually quite a number of studies were completed in sites with fairly high levels of implementation. El-Nemr (1979) concentrated his analysis on the teaching of biology as inquiry in high schools and colleges. He looked at the effects on achievement of information, on the development of process skills, and on attitudes toward science. The experimentally oriented biology curriculums achieved positive effects on all three outcomes. The average effect sizes were largest for process skills (0.44 at the high school level and 0.62 at the college level). For achievement they were 0.27 and 0.11 respectively, and for attitudes, 0.22 and 0.51. Bredderman's (1983) analysis included a broader range of science programs and included the elementary grades. He also reported positive effects for information (0.10), creativity (0.13), science process (0.52), and, in addition, reported effects on intelligence tests where they were included (0.50). From these and other studies we can conclude that it is possible to develop curriculums that will achieve model-relevant effects and also will increase learning of information and concepts. Also, vigorous curriculums in one area appear to stimulate growth in other, apparently unconnected areas. For example, Smith's (1980) analysis of aesthetics curriculums shows that the implementation of the arts-oriented curriculums was accompanied by gains in the basic skills areas. Possibly an active and effective curriculum in one area has energizing effects on the entire school program.

From the evidence in science and several other subject areas we conclude that curriculums can be constructed that can increase student learning. Also, they can be implemented, although not as easily as was believed twenty years ago. On the other hand, research on training has progressed substantially, so that we now know that we can engineer conditions that will implement the curriculums much more efficiently than was the case twenty years ago. The nature of the teaching skills is a blend of the interactive and the intellectual. Many require a high degree of skill in a variety of models of teaching. (See the skills described earlier in the review of theory-driven research.) Many also require mastery of an academic discipline. Fullan's (1982) argues persuasively that implementation requires a "deep understanding" of the curriculum itself-its rationale, process, structure, and materials.

There is little question that skills to use these curriculums require far more than ordinary knowledge and skills and therefore imply extensive training and practice. Spaulding's (1970) study asked important questions about the ability of teachers to implement a curriculum based on several theory-driven models of teaching well enough to achieve both general and model-relevant effects. The curriculum was designed for economically poor, socially disruptive, low-achieving elementary school students. It required teachers to master four teaching models and employ them selectively to achieve a complex set of goals. Social Learning Theory was employed to induce independent learning and socially integrative behavior. Inductive instructional methods were moderated by a cognitive-development frame of reference to define the learning tasks. The teachers had to comprehend and use social learning theory, inductive theory, and Piagetian cognitive psychology. Over a three-year period the students achieved greater personal control, integrative behavior, and academic achievement, and even measures of intelligence responded to the treatment. Spaulding's work underlines the skills of implementing a complex, theory-derived curriculum. The teachers had to be able to employ several theoretical frameworks. They had to be able to discriminate students on the basis of independence, social integration, achievement, and cognitive development. They had to be able to teach inductively, helping students gather, categorize, and label sets of data and to modify the processes of induction in accord with the characteristics of the students. Spaulding demonstrated that the teachers could acquire those skills and use them powerfully enough to reach a variety of goals.

For staff-development policy in school districts, the important message is that curriculums can make a difference and that some have been engineered and implemented that have made a large difference to students. Without a strong program in content, materials, and teaching process a poor level of implementation is likely to result (Hall, 1986; Hall & Loucks, 1977), which we will deal with in the following chapters.

STUDIES OF SCHOOLS THOUGHT TO BE EFFECTIVE

Research that compares schools has gone on for some time. In the early years, these studies were designed on a planned variation model, where schools operating from different stances toward education were compared with one another. For example, fifty years ago the beautifully designed "eight-year study" (Chamberlin & Chamberlin, 1943) submitted the theses of the Progressive movement to a serious (and generally successful) test and defended it against the suggestion that social and personal models of education were dangerous to the academic health of students. Twenty years ago the Coleman et al. study (1966) ushered in an era of investigation that continues, with the focus on naturalistic studies in which schools with unusually high achievement are compared with others. The Coleman et al. (1966) study was widely interpreted as indicating that variations between schools had little effect on student success because the ability and socioeconomic background of the students themselves were such powerful factors. Recent research on the differential effectiveness of schools (Brookover et al., 1978; Edmonds, 1979; Rutter et al., 1979) has called into question the findings of the Coleman study and advanced the methodology for studying schools. Although the study of effective schools has been criticized (Ralph & Fennessey, 1983; Rowen, Bossert, & Dwyer, 1983; Purkey & Smith, 1983) both on methodological grounds (studying the social and curricular organization of a school is complex and unwieldy) and in terms of its interpretation (can we use the characteristics of an outstanding school to make a mediocre one better?), the research continues and is making available to the field a much clearer set of hypotheses about how to approach the problem of increasing the positive impact of the school environment.

Research on effective schools is fueled by the belief that the realization of educational goals is achieved both by the organizational settings in which learning occurs as well as by the quality of specific curriculums and individual teachers. The focus is on the social organization of the school (the social climate) and curricular and instructional practices. Schools are first differentiated on a criterion of effectiveness, generally those aspects of academic achievement that are measured by mass administrations of commercially available tests. The researcher studies the schools and attempts to find out what accounts for the differences in productivity. Currently this work is evolving toward attempts to find causal connections by changing schools and trying to learn whether the changes are accompanied by changes in student achievement.

Several technical difficulties have confronted researchers studying schools for their effects on students. Little is known about the stability of either effectiveness or environments. Instrumentation is difficult and the logistics are even more complicated than the study of the classroom as a unit. However, recent investigations (Weil et al., 1984) have attacked these problems by studying schools that have been unusually effective for several years, comparing them with typical schools, and improving the reliability of instruments. The data base is new but promising. The first step is to learn how some schools achieve more than ordinary effects. The second is to learn how faculties, operating as a unit, can create energizing environments at the school level. These behaviors will compete for their place in preservice and inservice programs.

Many of the studies that have followed those by Brookover, Rutter, and their associates have oriented their search around the early findings. The result has been a body of studies that confirm many of the early results, which is useful because it suggests that the differences are in fact systemic. However, it is quite possible that there could be improvement in the definition of the variables or that other factors would emerge were they studied differently. Also, very little of the research has been oriented toward the potentially relevant concepts that are available from social psychology and organizational theory. Inclusion of these frames of reference might be worthwhile. The findings are emerging. Currently they fall in the following three areas:

School learning climate, including expectations and standards, clarity of mission, curricular organization, the monitoring of student progress, the reward structure, connectedness with the parents, and the provision of opportunities to learn.

School social climate, including a sense of community, student involvement in governance, orientation of the peer group, and provisions for orderliness and safety.

The role of the administrators also receives attention, active instructional leadership being stressed, as does the organizational climate of the school, with collaborative decision making receiving emphasis.

Although research on effective schools has a soft focus on the teacher behaviors that produce the conditions believed to be associated with effective school climates, we believe that they have to be taken seriously for a number of reasons. One is the size of the unit in question. Although the effect sizes are often small (about 0.10 in Weil's study) the number of students affected is very large. Second is the potential for interaction between school climate and many of the behaviors identified in the other lines of research. The power of curriculum and teaching may well be magnified by the climate of the school. Third, some of the conditions described in this research are very similar to those described by other lines of inquiry. (The production of an orderly, affirmative climate with clearly articulated goals and curriculum is an example.) Finally, the implementation of the skills derived from the other lines may well depend on the organizational factors that are emerging from the study of effective schools.

The research on models of teaching can provide direct assistance in defining relevant skills more clearly. The social and behavioral theories certainly promise methods for building social systems, methods that can be incorporated into preservice and inservice programs. Clearly the study of how to build effective school climates needs to be undertaken to define teachable skills further. Progress may be made relatively quickly if the current literatures on educational change (Fullan, 1982) and training (Joyce & Showers, 1983) are brought to bear. It may be that a major part of the skill in improving the educational climate may be in the management of educational change and the learning of new skills for implementing effective models of teaching. For the present the skills of working cooperatively to select the missions of the school and to think out how to create orderly yet stimulating environments appear to be essential. These skills are manifested in the role of faculty member rather than the role of instructor.

STUDIES OF TEACHERS THOUGHT TO BE EFFECTIVE

The Anderson-Brewer (1939) studies are generally acknowledged to mark the beginning of the modern era of investigations that employ the paradigm where descriptions of teacher behavior (process) are collected and correlated with a measure of desired student behavior (product). They studied dominant and integrative behavior in early childhood settings and measured the effect of the actions of the teacher on the social behavior of the students. Their research is important both because it established that teachers' social behavior does influence their students and also because it made clear how subtle and intricate are the relationships between teachers and students. In the classrooms where teachers were more integrative the students found ways of behaving more integratively with their peers. In the classrooms where teachers were more dominating the students learned how to be more dominative toward one another. Over the years many frames of reference have been used to describe teacher-student interaction and a wide range of types of student learning have been included (Flanders, 1970; Medley, 1977; Medley & Mitzel, 1963; Rosenshine, 1971; Spaulding, 1970; and Stallings, 1979).

What distinguishes this research is the focus on naturally occurring classroom behaviors. The research begins with the measurement of student academic achievement or other categories of student learning (growth in self-concept, independence, etc.). The researcher may elect to study teachers whose students are at the high, middle, or low sectors of the distribution. An alternative is to study a fairly large sample of teachers and expect that variation in student achievement will occur naturally. The next step is to study teacher and/or student behavior in the instructional setting – usually the classroom. Classrooms manifesting different levels of achievement are then compared and the frequencies of teacher and student behavior are correlated with the measures of learning. The findings emerge from this analysis. If teacher behaviors are identified that appear to differentiate levels of student learning, the investigators may then proceed to an experimental mode (Good, Grouws, & Ebmeier, 1983; Stallings, Needels, & Stayrook, 1979). Teacher behaviors associated with higher rates of student achievement will be taught to teachers whose students typically manifest low or moderate achievement, in order to determine whether acquiring the ability to manifest the behaviors will raise student learning. If the results of the experimental phase are positive, the teacher behaviors that differentiate the more from less effective teachers qualify as candidates for teachable teaching skills.

The naturalistic studies can be difficult to carry out. Access to the teachers and students has to be arranged and substantial amounts of classroom observation are necessary. The problem of stability both of effectiveness (Brophy & Evertson, 1974; Medley, Soar, & Coker, 1984) and behavior (Shavelson & Dempsey-Atwood, 1980) has been vexing. From year to year, teachers have their ups and downs in terms of the achievement that occurs in their students, and the researcher has to be careful because the apparently successful teacher in one year may be associated with only modest results the next. (Stability coefficients average only about .20.) Similarly, teachers' patterns of behavior change, causing us to modify our conception of what worked for those teachers. Also, what works for one may not always work for another.

From the standpoint of management, successful research often requires entry to the classrooms of very ineffective teachers, many of whom may experience acute discipline problems. The incidence of discipline problems also confronts the researcher with the problem of differentiating those aspects of teacher behavior that are related to the discipline problems from those that may be associated with the effectiveness of instruction per se. However, the paradigm for the research is straightforward and provides a relatively clear path to the findings, and the problems have not prevented energetic and well-organized researchers from carrying out some large and complex studies. The results are providing some promising avenues for staff development. It is important to note that all of the studies that have successfully differentiated more and less effective teachers have reported that effectiveness is the product of a complex of behaviors, rather than the use of a few practices. As we will see, some of the behaviors are relatively easy for teachers to learn and others appear to be much more difficult. Because of the complexity of the research and its yield we will need to deal with a number of investigations in order to get a useful picture of the findings.

The focus of naturalistic research on teaching is based on what teachers do in regular classrooms. Many of the studies focus on the management of instruction — what teachers do to prevent discipline problems and how they respond to them when they do occur, the arrangement and organization of materials, the time allotted to various activities and subjects, etc. — as much as on the means of instruction — the kinds of information provided and questions asked, the types of activities provided. The patterns of management and teaching employed by more successful teachers, that is, by teachers whose students score higher on standardized achievement tests, are often then collected into prescriptions or treatments and tested in experimental studies of teaching effectiveness.

Many of the naturalistic studies have been conducted in low-SES, primary classrooms (Stallings & Kaskowitz, 1972-1973; Soar, 1973) and elementary classrooms (Good, Grouws, & Ebmeier, 1983; Anderson, Evertson, & Brophy, 1979; Crawford et al., 1978; Evertson et al., 1980; Fisher et al, 1980; McDonald & Elias, 1976). There are a few studies in junior high classrooms (Evertson et al., 1980; Good, Grouws, & Ebmeier, 1983), and a handful with high school teachers of remedial subjects (Stallings, Needels, & Stayrook, 1979).

The teacher behaviors, practices, and skills that emerged from naturalistic studies of teaching generally relate more to the management of instruction than to actual instructional behaviors, although an important finding concerns the *amount* of instructional behavior used in teaching episodes. (Some of the less effective teachers apparently provide little instruction and rely on "seatwork" and other assignments to do the instructing for them.) Teacher practices recommended by several investigators (Brophy & Evertson, 1974; Good, Grouws, & Ebmeier, 1983; Fisher et al., 1980; Soar, 1973; Stallings & Kaskowitz, 1972-1973) include the teaching of students in large groups, allocation of time to academic tasks, the maintenance of highly-structured learning environments that reduced student off-task behaviors, the supervision or monitoring of "seatwork," and the regular assigning of homework. The pattern of teaching represented by this cluster of behaviors is often referred to as "direct instruction," which generally implies a clear presentation of goals, instruction over those goals, and the provision of practice in the classroom and/or in assignments to be accomplished out of school, and the monitoring of that practice with direct corrective feedback over work to be accomplished. There have been some fairly consistent findings for teacher practices with young, low-SES students. Stallings & Kaskowitz (1972-1973), in their correlational study of Follow Through first and third grade classrooms, found higher reading and math scores associated with structured, systematic instruction patterns (e.g., longer amounts of time spent on reading and math, direct instruction from teacher with praise and/or feedback). More flexible, less structured classrooms had somewhat lower scores in reading and math, although students in those classrooms had higher attendance rates, exhibited more independence, scored higher on problem-solving tests, and were more likely to take responsibility for their successes. The less structured classrooms were characterized by less direct instruction from teachers. Teachers in these classrooms spent greater amounts of time organizing the instructional environment with which students interacted, and in one-to-one interactions with children. Not every investigator has produced confirming results. For example, Flanders (1970) reported that the less structured, more "indirect" classrooms generated better results in both achievement and social behavior.

Some investigators have differentiated among types of student achievement. In another study of Follow Through kindergarten and first grade classrooms, Soar (1973) examined teacher behaviors with two types of student learning, which he called complex-abstract and simple-concrete. Simple-concrete gains were positively associated with teachers' direct time on academic activities; the asking of direct, narrow questions; large-group instruction; initiation of verbal interactions; and provision of praise and positive feedback. Soar also noted, however, a curvilinear relationship between teacher behavior and types of learning outcomes. He found moderately high levels of freedom facilitated complex growth while greater teacher direction increased simple learning. Both Soar and Stallings conducted extensive classroom observations with quite different observation instruments. Although results from the Beginning Teacher Evaluation Study (Phase II) (McDonald & Elias, 1976) were mixed, BTES (Phase III) (Fisher et al, 1980) replicated Stallings' and Soar's Follow Through findings in grades two and five. Teacher behaviors or practices associated with greater student achievement in reading and math included teacher accuracy in diagnosis, prescription of tasks related to students achievement level, substantive (academic) interaction with students, academic feedback, structuring, and clear directions.

As some of the investigators identified teacher practices that appeared to be associated with the achievement of low-SES students in reading and mathematics they proceeded to experiments to see if they could help teachers increase student achievement by using those practices. Two examples of this experimental work are Anderson, Evertson, and Brophy's (1979) experiment in first-grade reading and Good, Grouws, and Ebmeier's (1983) experiment in fourth-grade mathematics.

The Anderson, Evertson, and Brophy (1979) experimental study in first-grade reading was conducted over a period of months with middle-class students. A manual describing 22 principles of instruction thought to be effective for small-group instruction in the early grades was distributed to the 17 treatment teachers. The manual was described to teachers as a "set of guidelines for teacher management of reading group instruction" (p. 195). No additional training was provided the experimental group. The principles dealt with management of the group as a whole and the responses that teachers gave in feedback to students' answers. Mean reading scores at the end of the experiment for the observed and unobserved treatment groups were 57.09 and 59.81 as compared with a mean score of 50.90 for the control groups. The superior performance of treatment-teachers' students was attributed to teacher process variables, some of which could be attributed to the experimental treatment (e.g., efficient transitions, appropriate seating, use of overviews, minimizing choral responses, using ordered turns to select respondents, moderate and specific use of praise). Practices most likely to be implemented were those that "specifically described the skills... focused on behaviors that were familiar to the teachers... and had a rationale based on other classroom processes or student outcomes that made sense to teachers" (p. 219).

Good, Grouws, and Ebmeier (1983) did a series of experiments. The first, in the teaching of fourth-grade math, was conducted with relatively low-SES students. Twenty-one teachers read a manual that described the treatment practices (e.g., daily review, development of new content, seatwork, homework) that had been identified as contributing to student learning in the naturalistic study. Two 90-minute sessions were held with teachers to assure that they understood the recommended practices. Implementation by treatment teachers was high, with the exception of the "development" behavior advocated for 20 minutes per session. At the end of the two and one-half month experiment, students of experimental teachers performed significantly better than control teachers' students on math computation and showed no difference in problem solving. In some subsequent studies few effects were observed.

We believe that some of the practices identified by the naturalistic studies of teaching do not require extensive training. Others do. Although Stallings' work with secondary teachers is an exception, treatments have often consisted of providing teachers with a manual explaining the desired behaviors and in some cases a brief discussion of those behaviors (e.g., Good, Grouws, & Ebmeier, 1983; Crawford et al., 1978). The ease of training and implementation of these behaviors should not be surprising, however, when remembering that the behaviors were first identified among the practices of many classroom teachers teaching as they normally taught. The most difficult skills for teachers to acquire are those involving instruction to the whole class or small groups. Teachers who use the "truncated" recitation, that is, who rely heavily on seatwork and instructional materials to do the teaching, have a relatively difficult time learning how to conduct instruction.

The naturalistic study of teaching has provided a rich storehouse of effective practices for the management of instruction and student behavior and has demonstrated the relative ease of instructing teachers to use these practices. Future work in this area will need to address the generalizability of these findings to older and higher SES students in areas other than reading and math. However, this work has already been begun, with promising results with older students. Perhaps more productive may be the wedding of this work to that of the theory-based instruction researchers, who have concentrated heavily on the process and content of instruction for multiple purposes.

Most of the naturalistic studies have provided guidelines about how to conduct instruction in classrooms where the most frequent teaching episode has clear objectives and the teacher presents material and has the students either practice skills or study the material and then discuss it or recite it under the guidance of the teacher. This constitutes what we have called the basic recitation mode of teaching. The more effective teachers:

- Teach the classroom as a whole
- Present information or skills clearly and animatedly
- Keep the teaching sessions task-oriented
- Are nonevaluative and keep instruction relaxed
- Have high expectations for achievement (give more homework, pace lessons faster, create alertness)
- Relate comfortably to the students, with the consequence that they have fewer behavior problems

These behaviors are similar to those advocated by Hunter (1981), whose ITIP program stresses clear goals, affirmation toward students, closely monitored practice and homework, and direct, objectives-related feedback.

It is important to understand that the practices identified through the naturalistic research paradigm are those already used by the more effective teachers. Those more effective teachers do not need training in those practices, since they already use them. The greatest benefit will accrue when the least effective teachers, perhaps twenty-five or thirty percent, receive training in these practices. Even then, the assumption that student achievement will automatically rise cannot be made. An intensive three-year program to teach teachers a range of practices that appear supported by the naturalistic studies recently resulted in little or no effect on student achievement. In fact, the untreated control group actually exceeded the experimental group by the end of the third year (Slavin, 1986). Changing teaching practice is a delicate matter and increasing the frequency of use of certain practices may not have much effect unless they are employed appropriately and powerfully.

The interpretation of the results also has to be made carefully. As data analysis becomes more sophisticated some of the early findings are being reinterpreted by some researchers. For example, Lara and Medley (1987) noticed that most naturalistic studies have used class means as the measure of student achievement. Essentially, classes are tested before and after the period of observation and the average gain is computed. Lara and Medley

hypothesized that the same behaviors might have different effects on high-
and low-achieving students and they added to their analysis a comparison
of students more than a standard deviation above and below the mean. Their
results are striking. A number of behaviors helped either high or low
achievers but had no or even a *negative* effect on the other group. For
example, the provision of clear, explicit instructions helped low achievers but
had no effect on high achievers. Praise and rewards, which are often
associated with moderate class mean gains were *negatively* correlated with
both high and low achievers. Their analysis adds no clear evidence that the
interaction between teachers and students is very complex. Conceivably
the *most* effective teachers may turn out to be those who do not simply use
certain practices regularly, but those who modulate those practices in such a
way that they create more energy for learning across the spectrum of
individual differences. We need to be careful that we do not advocate
practices that appear to raise the average but which actually disadvantage
certain categories of students.

SUMMARY

The message of this chapter are that there are quite a number of educational
practices, ranging across ways of managing students and learning
environments, teaching strategies or models of teaching, curriculum
designs, dimensions of the learning environments of schools, and the use of
technologies, that can affect student learning. In our opinion, this array of
tested alternatives should be part of the substance of a human resource
development system. Improving student achievement should always be
receiving major attention within the system. We also stress that very few
practitioners currently have mastered and, therefore, cannot use many of the
practices described above. We are frequently surprised when we find that
district policymakers believe that somehow, without training, teachers and
administrators have developed a wide range of strategies. Rather, most
teachers use a very narrow range of practices (Sirotnik, 1983; Goodlad &
Klein, 1970; Medley, 1977) and expand that repertoire only when substantial
and carefully designed training is provided.

CHAPTER FIVE

CONTENT FOR THE SUBSTANTIVE COMPONENTS OF THE SYSTEM

We need now to bring together the material presented in chapters two, three, and four before proceeding in the following chapters to the design of training itself. Essentially, we need to consider the selection of the content for each of the substantive components – the individual (oriented toward teachers as individuals and in peer-coaching teams); the collective (oriented toward schools and sections of schools); and the systemic (oriented toward the implementation of district-sponsored initiatives).

As we deal with the process of selecting content we make the assumption that the organizational structures suggested in chapters two and three are in place. That is, all teachers are members of study groups (about six persons in each group) and within those can engage in peer-coaching relationships with other members of the groups. Within each school the group leaders are organized in a school improvement committee and within the district, or clusters of schools in the case of large districts, representatives from each school improvement council are organized in a district or cluster staff development council. Within this organizational structure the content for each of the substantive components is selected and the programs are brought into existence.

An important duty of the district committee is to engage in the study of alternatives – the   kind of material we have just discussed in chapter four — and bring information to school councils and, through them, to study groups. As our process unfolds, informed decision making will be critical, for people can scarcely select options unless they know about them. As this is written, many teachers, schools, and school districts are not studying alternatives that would have great promise for them, simply because the information about those alternatives has not been made available.

SUBSTANCE FOR THE INDIVIDUAL COMPONENT

The individual component is made up of an array of workshops and courses that teachers will select on the basis of their perception about what will benefit them and, through them, their students. The decision-making process needs to identify substantive candidates for the array and to make selections, get them operating, and enable teachers to enroll for them.

We suggest that three procedures be employed concurrently to generate the candidates for the array — procedures that tap teachers' perceptions of substance that will benefit them, perceptions of substance that teachers and other staff have the capability of offering to one another, and items created through research and development activities of the types described in chapter four.

Perceptions of Need or Potential Benefit

These are obtained through the procedure that has become known throughout the profession as the "needs survey." Essentially, all teachers are asked to scrutinize their curricular and instructional practices (what they teach, how they teach, and the instructional materials they use) and indicate whether there is content, teaching skills and strategies, or materials that they would like to study because they believe it would improve the quality of their instruction. It is important that people take a hard look at *all* the courses and curriculum areas they teach and that they consider content needs as well as needs for teaching and materials. In responding, each teacher looks at his or her content areas (for elementary teachers, content will include all of the basic curriculum areas — reading, arithmetic, science, social studies, language arts) and answers the questions, Can I think of any materials, knowledge of content, or instructional skills that would help me do a better job in this area? Which ones would have the highest priority for me?

The study group leaders organize the product and take it to the school council, which further organizes it and forwards it to the district or cluster committee. That committee now has the task of sorting out the items that have been suggested and formulating what we will call the Teacher Request List.

Potential Offerrer Perceptions

This procedure centers on identifying potential offerrers of service – teaching and administrative personnel and persons from local universities, teacher centers, intermediate agencies, and professional organizations. The personnel are asked if they are prepared to offer service to others and what it might be. They are asked to recommend others who might offer service. University departments, not only in education but in academic areas, are asked if they would like to provide service. The district committee asks school councils to canvass their personnel and approaches the other agencies and departments in the district for their ideas. The resulting product is added to the Teacher Request List and the lists of requests and offerrers are compared as well to determine which of the requests from the survey of perceived needs can be matched with a potential offerrer.

The Study of Suggestions from Research and Development

The study by the district council of alternatives from research and development should result in a third list of possibilities that can be compared with the other lists. For example, it is useful to learn how potential offerrers line up with suggested content and with researched alternatives, for it allows us to see the feasibility of matching perceived needs with high-impact options for which potential staff are available (see Table 1).

Nonetheless the entire organized list is now sent back to the teachers to ascertain their perception of priorities. In addition to items that an individual has contributed in the early round of expression of needs and wants, each person now examines what has been suggested by others, potential offerrers, and the district committee. At this stage each person is asked to examine the entire list and indicate what has the greatest appeal to them as individuals.

With that information in hand the council sets to work to assemble the offerings that will be made. Some popular items may have to be shelved because providers are not available. The council will consider whether to locate offerrers in some of those areas for the future, or to develop trainers by finding interested people and obtaining training for them. Time is a consideration – some promising ideas may require more time than can be feasibly arranged or some of the more extensive items may have to be saved for another year.

The eventual array should have a balance among the study of teaching skills and strategies, content, and the exploration of instructional materials. Some items should be included that help people enhance their existing repertoire and some items should provide the opportunity for the learning of new material. Many districts reserve some places for items of personal

TABLE 1. POTENTIAL OFFERINGS SUGGESTED FROM SURVEYS
AND STUDY (A PARTIAL LIST)

	Sources		
Areas Suggested	Teacher Requests	Provider Suggested	Council Study
Classroom management	25	2	+
TESA	15	4	+
Writing across the curriculum	15	2	+
Computer software	18	6	
Computer programing	10	4	
Word processing	45	0	+
Film as literature	00	1	
Laboratory science	1	1	+
Effective schools	10	0	+ +

interest (such as personal finance) and possibilities of attendance at interesting conferences.

SELECTING CONTENT FOR
THE COLLECTIVE COMPONENT

The key to the selection of the content for the school-based component is the organization of the faculty to select areas for improving the quality of education in the school (Joyce, Hersh, & McKibbin, 1983). Collective action is the key. The same sources of ideas are available as in the generation of content possibilities for the individual component, except that the consideration is not the provision of service to individuals but for the faculty as a whole. In the past the distinction between the individual and the school has not always been clear. We have observed districts where resources have been provided to schools but used as if individual preferences were the key, generating opportunities for individuals as volunteers rather than common directions with a commitment by all.

Thus, the school committee leads the faculty through a process parallel to the one described just above. Individual faculty are asked to contribute ideas. Possibilities from research and development are examined and discussed. The research on effective schools has many possibilities. Recent innovations in the school program are examined—in many schools the computer is still an innovation and may bear collective action. The curriculum areas are examined to determine whether any can stand improvement.

The list of possibilities will grow and needs to be narrowed eventually until just a few items remain—items that are feasible because they are perceived to be important by a majority of the faculty and the means are available to support them.

Some of the options we have observed (see Table 1) include:

- *The study of the social climate of the school.* This study uses the research on schools thought to be effective as a guide for the development of programs designed to improve aspects of the climate. This type of activity generally requires consultant service, although there are a few districts where all the principals have prepared themselves to lead the process of improving school climates.
- *The renovation of a curriculum area.* In elementary schools the generalist teacher provides most of the instruction in the basic areas and it can be argued that some area should always be in a process of renovation. Reading, language arts and literature, social studies, science, arithmetic, and the other areas are candidates. Generally the curriculum areas are not in equally good shape and it is not difficult to find one that could

bear improvement. In secondary schools the offerings by grade are often convenient foci. For example, in one year freshman courses might be considered; in another, advanced placement courses; in another, the articulation of courses within a subject. Cross-subject strategies are also feasible. For example, reading and writing in the content areas has been a popular staff development focus for some faculties.

- *Teaching and learning strategies.* A faculty can take a strategy, such as cooperative learning, mnemonics, or one of the other models discussed in chapter four, and study and learn to use it together. Some faculties are currently studying ways of teaching every subject in such a way that the thinking ability of the students is improved (Perkins, 1986; Costa, 1985). It is feasible for people to add one or two teaching strategies to their repertoire in any given year. The available alternatives are numerous enough to provide options for instructional improvement for many years.
- *Technology.* We have already mentioned computers. The use of videotape and broadcast television are other applications of technology to instruction. Some schools have positively impacted their instructional programs by incorporating resource-based offerings for their students, thus enabling the study of topics and courses that cannot be offered by the faculty. In small high schools, for example, the number of offerings is necessarily limited and resource-based courses provide many additional opportunities (Joyce, Hersh, & McKibbin, 1983, chap. ten).
- *The learning styles of students.* Some faculties have engaged in the study of stylistic differences and how to accommodate to them by providing instructional variants (Spaulding, 1970; Hunt, 1971; Dunn & Dunn, 1975). This provides a very nice avenue for faculties just starting to learn how to work together.
- *Attending to special populations.* Population-oriented initiatives for school improvement have become popular in recent years as the states and the federal government have provided resources for students having special needs (generally known as "special education"), students of varying cultural backgrounds, students believed to have special talents, bilingual students, and so on. Most of these initiatives are difficult to implement properly. "Pull-out" programs, in which students are removed from "regular" class for special attention, have been particularly unsatisfactory, because they disrupt continuity and often generate fragmented programs for the students in question. Many of these programs need attention.

The school council needs to lead the faculty to a narrowing of the list of possibilities and the selection of the one or two areas that will receive attention during any given year. It is *very* important for the focus to be narrowed. There is a tendency to get too many projects going at once, with the result that none get done well.

As each school settles on its candidates for improvement efforts, these need to be forwarded to the district committee which then has the task of trying to find staff development support for the initiatives. They need to search for consultants and instructional personnel from the same sources that are tapped for the clinical component. Possibly teachers from some of the schools can obtain training that they can bring back to their faculties. Possibly the district cadre needs to consider some of the suggested areas. The committee also needs to assess costs and decide how much assistance can be given to particular schools. The eventual decisions need to be a result of negotiation.

THE SYSTEMIC COMPONENT

Most districts have not been organized to accompany system-wide initiatives in curriculum, instruction, or technology, with the staff development to ensure a healthy implementation (Fullan & Pomfret, 1977; Fullan & Park, 1981; Hall, 1986; Crandall et al., 1982; Miles & Huberman, 1984; Joyce, Hersh, & McKibbin, 1983). In the area of curriculum, for example, it has been thoroughly demonstrated that district committees can produce curriculum guides and order and deliver to classrooms textbooks and other materials, but that implementation, including the use of new textbooks in many cases, often doesn't occur because the staff development component has not been extensive enough. There are two reasons for this state of affairs. One is that educators simply have not understood the amounts and types of study that are necessary for people to learn how to employ new procedures and often new content in the classroom (see chapters six and seven). The second is that it is difficult to make the hard decisions to narrow the district focus in any given period. Ideas for school improvement abound and it is not uncommon for districts to have a dozen or two initiatives going at one time, none of them supported substantially enough for a systemic implementation. Coordination has been a problem. We have observed all too many districts where a large number of departments or other organizational units generate initiatives without the knowledge that their opposite numbers are generating similar ones. Thus the curriculum units, departments of elementary, secondary, and special education, staff development offices, departments serving the gifted and talented, and many others generate initiatives and communicate them to schools and teachers "willy-nilly."

The answer we propose is to replicate the process we have described above for identifying the focus of school-based initiatives but with the purpose of identifying the one or two important initiatives that will have center stage in the district for a year or two. Teachers, study groups, schools, and committee members need to put forth their candidates. Lists need to be developed and culled. The committee needs to ask whether the district has unfinished business with past initiatives or has committed to expenditures for facilities and equipment that will not be used well without staff development. Have videotape machines been purchased for schools? How is the computer doing? Have additions been made to the library or has it acquired access to electronic libraries or become stocked with self-instructional programs?

Essentially the list we generated when thinking about the possibilities for schools can serve the same purpose when thinking about the district. Curriculum, technology, teaching skills and strategies, social climate, can all become a focus in the larger organization.

It is within the schools that the district initiatives will have their implementation, so communication is essential during the decision-making process and in the planning of implementation. For example, were a teaching strategy like cooperative learning to become a district focus, the result would be training for a large number of people in many sites and much hard work in every school to implement the strategy. Or if school social climate became the focus, then all school faculties would have to learn to examine their social climates and make plans for improvements. It may be that many districts would be wise to plan their initiatives no less than a year in advance so that they can develop the strong cadres that will be necessary to support the training.

SUMMARY

Content for the clinical, collective, and systemic components of staff development programs may be similar, that is, curriculum, instruction, technology, or learning styles might serve as the substance of study for individuals, school faculties, or entire districts. Decision-making processes for the various components, however, will vary with their goals. Individuals will be evaluating personal needs while schools and districts will determine needs for groups of students. Adequate training will be the key to the success of all three components. Hence, let us turn our attention to the design of training and to the research that now enables us to plan staff development programs that have a very high probability of succeeding.

CHAPTER SIX

THE DESIGN OF TRAINING: PROVIDING THE CONDITIONS FOR LEARNING

Let us focus for a moment on a study group of science teachers in a pair of middle schools somewhere in the Midwest.

The six teachers are concentrating on increasing the teaching of scientific thinking as part of their courses. They have chosen the Inquiry Training model of teaching (Joyce & Weil, 1986, chap. five) as the focus of their effort. The model is specifically designed to teach causal reasoning. When using it the teachers present puzzling situations to the students who attack the problem by collecting and analyzing data and developing and testing hypotheses.

The teachers have attended a workshop where they studied the theory of inquiry training, participated in demonstrations where they were led through the process, analyzed videotapes of teaching episodes, and practiced formulating problems, presenting them to one another, and leading the inquiry training process. For the last two weeks they have been practicing the model with their students, teaching them how to analyze the problems, to collect and organize information, to build concepts and hypotheses, and test them. The teachers have worked together to build sets of puzzling problems that fit the content of the courses they teach and are now analyzing their students' ability to collect relevant information and organize it. For the time being the focus of their peer observations is on students ask to gain information. The focus of the study group meetings is on ways of helping the students work together to formulate better questions.

Our goal is the design of training that enables people to learn knowledge and skills new to them and transfer that knowledge and skill to active classroom practice. In this chapter we will examine research on training for two purposes. The first is to find principles for designing programs that will result in high levels of skill and its implementation. The second is a search for ways of conducting training in such a way that it increases the aptitude to learn skills more easily and effectively. In other words, we want to design training so that people learn to become more effective learners. As we did in chapter four, we will often report results in effect sizes (standard deviation units) to make comparisons between treatments more clear.

SELECTING TRAINING OBJECTIVES

What do we expect good training to accomplish? Aside from the content – academic knowledge, approaches to curriculum and instruction, how students develop and learn, learning styles, technologies, etc. – what is the nature of the behavior necessary to put that content into work in the classroom?

Training Content

Figure 3 illustrates the range of possibilities for selecting training objectives. The left side of the matrix defines characteristics of the training content. If the substance of the training is knowledge and skill that teachers generally possess to some extent but which need refinement for optimal classroom use, decision makers will be working in the top half of the matrix. For example, training that focusses on teacher praise and encouragement of student work or time allowed students to respond to questions would be classified as "refining of existing skill." Presumably, teachers already provide verbal encouragement to students for their efforts and ask questions during classroom recitations. The object of training becomes a more appropriate use of existing behaviors. If, on the other hand, training content represents for teachers an addition to repertoire – knowledge and skill not currently known about or practiced in their instruction – the bottom half of the matrix will be used. Obviously, "new repertoire" must be defined in relation to the knowledge and skills of individuals – what is new to one person may exist in the repertoire of another. Research on classroom teaching, however, has fairly well described how most teachers teach and we can be fairly certain that few teachers use the

Figure 3. Decision -making Matrix: Selecting Training
Objectives.

Content Definition	Training Outcomes			
	Awareness/ Knowledge	Attitude Change	Skill Development	Transfer of Training
	Theories, Practices, Curriculums	Self, Children, Academic Content	Discrete Behaviors, Strategies	Consistent Use, Appropriate Use
Refining of Existing Knowledge and Skills: Simple Complex				
Addition to Repertoire: Simple Complex				

curricular and instructional models described in chapter four, (e.g., the more complex varieties of cooperative learning and group investigation, key-word and link-word memory strategies, synectics, inductive thinking) (Sirotnik, 1983; Medley, 1977; Goodlad & Klein, 1970; Good, Grouws, & Ebmeier, 1983, etc.).   On the other hand, most teachers praise students, correct them, orient students to lessons, provide practice in class and as homework, so training that concentrates on those practices is for most persons an elaboration and strengthening of existing practices.

In addition to deciding whether training content will be a refining of existing knowledge and skill or an addition to repertoire, designers should also estimate the difficulty level of knowledge and skills to be learned. Placing content on a simple/complex continuum will clarify later decisions about the intensity and duration of training experiences.

Types of Outcomes

The outcomes expected of training have implications both for the design and evaluation of training. Potential outcomes are:

1. The knowledge or awareness of educational theories and practices, new curriculums, or academic content
2. Changes in attitudes toward self (role perception changes), children (minorities, handicapped, gifted), academic content (attitudes toward science, English as a second language, math)
3. Development of skill (the ability to perform discrete behaviors such as designing and delivering questions of various cognitive levels or the ability to perform clusters of skills in specific patterns as in a synectics exercise)
4. Transfer of training and "executive control" (the consistent and appropriate use of new skills and strategies for classroom instruction)

Given the objectives of any element of a program, the next task is to design training for maximum probability that the desired effects will be achieved.

Training Components

Several training elements are at our disposal.

An exploration of theory through discussions, readings, lectures, etc. is necessary for an understanding of the rationale behind a skill or strategy and the principles that govern its use. Study of theory facilitates skill acquisition by increasing one's discrimination of the demonstrations, by providing a mental image to guide practice and clarify feedback, and by promoting the attainment of executive control.

The **demonstration** or modeling of skill greatly facilitates learning. Skills can be demonstrated in settings that simulate the workplace, mediated through film or videotape, or conducted live in the training setting. Demonstrations can be mixed with explanation; the theory and modelling components need not be conducted separately. In fact, they have reciprocal effects. Mastery of the rationale of the skill facilitates discrimination, and modeling facilitates the understanding of underlying theories by illustrating them in action.

The third training component is the **practice** of skill under simulated conditions. The closer the training setting approximates the workplace the more transfer is facilitated. Considerable amounts of skill can be developed, however, in settings far removed from and different from the workplace.

"Peer teaching" (practice with other teachers) even has advantages. It provides experience as a "student", enables trainees to profit from one another's ideas and skill, and clarifies mistakes. It also is a good arrangement in which to develop the skills of peer coaching. Peer teaching and practice with small groups of children are safer settings for exploration than a full classroom. How much practice is needed depends, of course, on the complexity of the skill. To bring a model of teaching of medium complexity under control requires twenty or twenty-five trials in the classroom over a period of about eight or ten weeks. The more simple skills, or those more similar to previously developed ones, will require less practice to develop and consolidate than those that are more complex or different from the teachers' current repertoire.

Finally, **feedback** about performance facilitates skill development. Trainees can learn to provide feedback to each other and, utilizing audio or video recording, can critique themselves once they have a clear idea of the skill and how to use it. Feedback from others, to be of maximum utility for skill development, should occur as soon as possible following practice, should be specific to the behaviors being attempted by the trainee, and should be nonevaluative. Feedback will be discussed in greater detail in chapter seven.

The **coaching** of teaching occurs in the workplace following initial training. Coaching provides support for the community of teachers attempting to master new skills, provides technical feedback on the congruence of practice trials with ideal performance, and provides companionship and colleagial problem solving as new skills are integrated with existing behaviors and implemented in the instructional setting. Coaching will also be discussed at length in chapter seven.

Research on Training

Training, of course, does not exist outside a context. Someone has to decide what will be the substance of the training, who will provide training, when and where the training will be held and for what duration. The norms of the workplace impinge on the receptivity of participants to various configurations of training experiences, as do labor-relations histories and interpersonal relationships among participants. We have less data on the impact of many of these environmental and governance variables on the effectiveness of training than we have on actual training components. However, we recommend the participatory governance modes described in chapters two, three, and five to increase understanding of both the content and why it was selected for each component. Also, as we discussed in chapter three, we believe that cohesiveness and strong leadership in the school are critical to the success of training. The best trainers, working with the most relevant and powerful content, will find little success or receptivity in poor organizational climates. However, good climates and high motivation will not substitute for well-designed training. Fortunately, that research and experience have reached the point where we can assert that for specific training outcomes, certain training components or combinations of components provide optimal conditions for learning. Essentially, nearly all teachers can master a very wide range of teaching skills and strategies provided that the training is well-designed and the climate of the school facilitates and promotes cooperative study and practice.

Hence, designers of training must answer several questions before planning any training experience. For whom is the training intended and what is expected to result from the training? Is follow-up to training built into schools as a permanent structure or must follow-up be planned and delivered as part of the training package? Does the content of the training represent new learning for participants or is it an attempt to refine existing knowledge and skills?

Also, designers need to decide which training components will be used and how they will be combined. These components include the presentation of information or theory about the topic of the training, live and mediated demonstration or modelling of new skills and teaching models, opportunities for practice of new skills and strategies in the training setting as well as in the workplace, and feedback on performance in practice trials. Peer coaching of new skills and strategies, which largely occurs in the workplace, ideally is taught and practiced in the training setting as well.

Research on training provides some interesting insights into the efficacy of various training components and, particularly, combinations of them (Bennett, 1987; Joyce & Showers, 1983) (see Table 2). Information or theory-only treatments increase knowledge by about ES 0.50 (0.5 of a standard deviation on a normal curve), whereas theory combined with demonstration, practice and feedback results in an ES of 1.31 for knowledge (Bennett, 1987).

When skill is the desired outcome of training, the advantage of the combinations is equally clear. Theory or demonstration alone result in effect sizes for skill of around .5 of a standard deviation for refining existing skills, lower for new skills. Theory, demonstration and practice combined result in an ES of approximately .7 for skill, whereas theory, demonstration, practice, and feedback combined result in an ES of 1.18. When in-class coaching is added to the theory, demonstration, practice, feedback treatment, skill continues to rise.

Strangely, the question of transfer of training has been asked much less frequently in research on training than has the question regarding skill

Table 2. Effect Sizes for Training Outcomes by Training Components

Training Components and Combinations	Training Outcomes		
	Knowledge	Skill	Transfer of Training
Information	.63	.35	.00
Theory	.15	.50	.00
Demonstration	1.65	.26	.00
Theory Demo.	.66	.86	.00
Theory Practice	1.15		.00
Theory Demo. Prac.		.72	.00
Theory Demo. Practice Feedback	1.31	1.18	.39
Theory Demo. Practice Feedback Coaching	2.71	1.25	1.68

acquisition. Consequently, many fewer studies of training have measured transfer effects than have measured skill acquisition. Perhaps the assumption has been that skill, once developed, would automatically be used in classroom instruction. Recent analyses of the literature on training confirm what many trainers, teacher educators, and supervisors have long suspected — transfer of learned knowledge and skill is by no means a sure bet. In studies that have asked the transfer question (e.g., did participants use new skills in the classroom, did they use them appropriately, did they integrate new skills with existing repertoire, was there long-term retention of the products of training), several findings emerge. First, the gradual addition of training elements does not appear to impact transfer noticeably (ES of .00 for information or theory; theory plus demonstration; theory, demonstration and feedback; ES of .39 for theory, demonstration, practice and feedback). However, a large and dramatic increase in transfer of training – ES 1.68 – occurs when in-class coaching is added to an initial training experience comprised of theory explanation, demonstrations, and practice with feedback.

We have concluded from these data that teachers can acquire new knowledge and skill and use it in their instructional practice when provided with adequate opportunities to learn. We have hypothesized, further, that fully elaborated training systems develop a "learning to learn" aptitude; that, in fact, individuals learn more efficiently over the long term by developing the metacognitions that enable self-teaching in settings where essential training elements are missing.

Implications for Staff Development Practice

We have drawn several conclusions from the research on training which have implications for staff development programs serving individuals, schools and systems:

- First, regardless of who initiates a training program, participants must have sufficient opportunity to develop skill that they can eventually practice in classroom settings
- Second, if the content of training is new to trainees, training will have to be more extensive than for substance that is relatively familiar
- Third, if transfer of training is the training objective, follow-up such as coaching in the workplace will probably be necessary

SKILLS TEACHERS NEED AS LEARNERS TO MASTER NEW KNOWLEDGE AND SKILLS

As research on effective teaching yields more data, it becomes increasingly urgent that teachers be able to use the products of that research. Designing training that maximizes opportunities for mastery of new information and skills is an important task. Are there "learning-to-learn" skills which some teachers develop in or bring to the training setting, and if so, can they be developed in others? And what have we learned from training about conditions that nurture and develop "learning-to-learn" skills?

Ripple & Drinkwater (1982, p. 1949) in their review of research on transfer of learning, note the following about "learning to learn":

The concept of learning-to-learn implies the development of strategies or learning sets as a result of such experience (practice with a variety of problems). Preliminary practice on tasks that will transfer positively to performance on different criterion tasks is required for the development of learning to learn strategies.

From research on training and curriculum implementation, school improvement and change, and our personal training experiences, we have identified several practices, attitudes, and skills that appear to facilitate learning apttitude.

Persistence

Practice of new skills and behaviors increases both skill and comfort with the unfamiliar. The benefits of practice are well known to educators and are often reiterated in training settings. Yet many trainees try a new skill or practice only once or else never try it at all. The "driving through" initial trials in which performance is awkward and effectiveness appears to decrease rather than increase is one characteristic which appears to differentiate successful from unsuccessful learners. Avoidance of the difficult and awkward is not unique to teachers as learners, as golfers, skiers and tennis players can attest. Changing one's own behavior is difficult, especially when one has fairly dependable strategies already fully developed.

Acknowledgment of the Transfer Problem

Mastery of new skills, especially when they differ substantially from existing skills, is rarely sufficient for implementation in classroom practice. Introducing a new procedure or teaching strategy into an existing repertoire of instructional behaviors generally creates dislocation and discomfort. Yet, considerable practice of new behaviors is required if teachers are not only to become technically proficient with them but also to integrate them sensibly and appropriately with existing behaviors. Teachers who understand the necessity for the additional effort required if new behaviors are to be merged with existing instructional practices and expend the extra effort to think through where the new behaviors fit and for what they are effective are much more likely to implement an innovation than teachers who don't acknowledge and address this learning task. Transfer of training is a separate learning task, a metacognitive condition that appears to increase efficiency in skill acquisition as well as eventual transfer of learning. Both trainers and learners have tended to underestimate the cognitive aspects of implementation – teachers have assumed they have only to see something in order to use it skillfully and appropriately, and trainers have devoted little or no time during training to attacking the transfer problem.

Teaching New Behaviors to Students

Part of the difficulty in introducing new curriculums or teaching processes into the classroom is student discomfort with change. Students quickly learn the rules of the classroom game and how to respond to the demands of the learning environment. Those who are successful with existing conditions may be particularly reluctant to have the rules changed. When new procedures are introduced, students may exert pressure on the teacher to return to the patterns of behavior with which they are familiar and comfortable, or, if not comfortable, which they understand well. Consequently, if a teacher has typically run a brisk recitation in which students were asked rapid-fire recall questions over material they have previously read or been introduced to in some other fashion, students have learned how to signal they know the answers, how to avoid being called on when they don't know the answers, and what to expect in terms of feedback (e.g., immediate information regarding the correctness of responses, the message that there is a "right" answer). If this teacher then introduces an inquiry process into the classroom which shifts responsibility to students for collecting and analyzing data and setting and testing hypotheses, and knowledge is viewed as emergent and tentative, student discomfort with the new demands may encourage the teacher to abandon the new strategy after one or two trials. When this happens, neither teacher nor students develop sufficient expertise with the new strategy to evaluate potential benefits and uses.

Teachers who directly teach the requisite skills to students, including both the cognitive and social tasks required by specific innovations, are much more likely to integrate successfully the new behaviors with existing instructional repertoire.

Meeting the Cognitive Demands of Innovations

Teachers frequently have complained that their training has over-emphasized "theory" and neglected the practical or clinical aspects of teaching. It is probable, however, that without a thorough grounding in the theory of an innovation, or what Fullan calls "deep understanding", that teachers will be unable to use new skills and strategies in any but a most superficial manner. Understanding of the theory underlying specific behaviors enables flexible and appropriate use of the behaviors in multiple situations and prevents the often ludicrous following of "receipes" for teaching. Thus, a teacher who wishes to organize presentations or entire courses with advance organizers must understand the conceptual framework of the material to be so organized and be able to extract and organize concepts into a hierarchy of ideas. The teacher who wishes to apply the link-work method to the acquisition of foreign language vocabulary must understand the research from cognitive psychology regarding the role of association in memory. And the teacher who wishes to implement a contingency management system must completely understand the nature of reinforcers and how they operate.

Teachers who master the theory undergirding new behaviors they wish to use in their classrooms implement those behaviors in greater congruence with the researched and tested ideal and are more likely to replicate results obtained in research settings with their own students.

Productive Use of Peers

During the last few years, research on training has documented the benefits of peers helping peers in the implementation of innovations. Regular, structured interaction between or among peers over substantive content is one of the hallmarks of a profession and is viewed by other professionals as essential professional nourishment rather than a threat to autonomy. A family dentist does not hesitate to consult a root canal specialist in the midst of an examination if he or she feels the need for consultation nor does a hairdresser feel constrained in getting a second opinion regarding the type of permanent needed for a particular head of hair. This propensity to seek the advice and assistance of other professionals was vividly illustrated recently when one of the leading cardiologists in the world explained to us his decision-making process in the operating room. Fifteen medical personnel (surgeons, anesthesiologists, cardiologists) discussed the pros and cons of reopening a patient's chest versus using drug therapy following by-pass surgery in which the patient's heart was fibrillating. Rather than feeling embarrassment that he had asked for other opinions, the cardiologist seemed to assume we would find comfort in the fact that he had consulted the other professionals on the spot.

Teachers also have begun to appreciate the benefits of mutual study and problem solving in relation to professional competence. The programs which build into training and follow-up of training opportunities for collegial work on the mastery and use of innovative practices and content contribute not only to the individual competence of teachers participating in them but also build their sense of membership in a profession. Furthermore, teachers who assume a proactive stance in relation to self-help peer relationships appear to gain much more from such programs than do teachers who merely "submit" to them. Observing other professionals work is a valuable learning experience in itself, and collaborative analysis of teaching and planning for appropriate use of an innovation usually results in more practice and more focussed practice. Finally, the proactive teachers who can and will state what they need — what they understand and what they don't — rather than relying on the mind-reading capability of their peers are likely to benefit more from professional collegial study than teachers who are passive in the relationship.

Flexibility

Flexibility appears to be a highly functional attribute of teachers in training. During the first stage of learning when trainees are introduced to new content and/or processes, traditional thinking about curriculum and instruction may have to be reoriented. If training consists of learning an inductive thinking strategy, for example, current materials may have to be reorganized or supplemented in order to provide students with data rather than conclusions and generalizations. Teachers may also have to rethink their roles as instructors in the classroom. If they have conceived their roles as information givers, instructional processes that transfer greater responsibility to students for their own learning may require rethinking of educational goals, ways and means. In the transfer stage of learning, when teachers are attempting to use new content and processes appropriately in the instructional setting, a reorientation to students may be necessary. When new and different expectations are held for students, teachers must figure out what learning skills students possess and which must be directly taught in order for students to operate within different frameworks. Teacher flexibility in the learning process can be summed up as a spirit of inquiry, a willingness to experiment with their own behavior, and an openness to evidence that alternatives have something to offer.

CONDITIONS THAT HELP TEACHERS DEVELOP LEARNING SKILLS

If indeed skills, attitudes and characteristics such as perserverence in the face of discomfort, understanding of the transfer of training problem, directly teaching new processes to students, understanding and tackling the cognitive demands of innovations, productive use of peers in the learning process, and teacher flexibility develop learning-to-learn capabilities, what are the conditions in inservice training programs that foster these aptitudes and behaviors?

Adequate Training

Training that develops a high degree of skill with and understanding of an innovation seems essential if teachers are to later practice new behaviors in their classrooms, teach new processes to students and work collaboratively with peers on appropriate implementation. Providing conditions that enable teachers to engage in learning-to-learn activities probably means designing training that includes an explication of theory, multiple demonstrations of processes and content to be mastered, and opportunities for practice with factual, non-evaluative feedback.

Opportunities for Colleagial Problem Solving

Working closely with peers is not characteristic of most higher education training programs and is definitely not typical of schools. The isolation in which teachers in our schools work has been well documented, and a perusal of most school's schedules would confirm what teachers tell us--teachers generally work alone in a classroom of students and see other teachers perhaps one period a day (secondary) if they go to a common room during their preparation period. Time for both preservice and inservice teachers to observe each other work, analyze their teaching, and plan together the best choices of content and process for specific educational objectives must be structured into the workplace.

Building Norms That Support Experimentation

Staff development programs frequently offer training that directs "Learn this and do it. Effective teachers do X." Teachers are told to provide positive reinforcement to students, assign homework, provide a learning "set", ask questions at varying levels of cognitive complexity, keep students on task, and evaluate student progress, and are given procedures for accomplishing these behaviors. If teachers were to learn, first in their preservice programs and later in their school districts that experimentation with one's own behavior can lead to increased knowledge, they would be more open to exploring alternatives. One of the greatest difficulties encountered by schoo improvement and change efforts is the attitude that "we already learned how to do that". This is not to label teachers as intransigent but rather to note that we have, through our most common approaches to teacher preparation and training, inculcated the notion that right answers are fight forever. To the extent that we can develop views of knowledge as emergent, views of the profession as changing, and views of the individual as growing, we will have provided conditions that enable teachers to experiment with the content and process of their craft.

Organizational Structures that Support Learning

Districts and schools can structure the workplace so that collaborative work is possible and rewarded, training is provided that maximizes opportunities for skill mastery and implementation, and attitudes and norms that support experimentation are communicated. Building level and central office administration are powerful (and sometimes unintentional) molders of expectations and norms, and dispensers of rewards and sanctions. Whether the belief is waranted or not, many teachers feel they are not free to experiment with curriculum and instruction, that the "knowledge of most worth" is that covered by standardized tests. The forceful and active leadership of school and district admninistrators can counter prevailing norms and help establish new ones.

IMPLEMENTING TRAINING DESIGNS

Returning to Opal District, which we discussed in chapter two, what are the training implications for Adrienne as an individual working on her clinical skills, as a member of a coaching team and study group working on a school improvement goal, and as a teacher in a district attempting to improve student writing through the use of computer-assisted word processing?

Adrienne and her colleagues possess nearly all the attitudes, skills, and practices discussed above. Because of their commitment to collaborative approaches to educational problems, they have a framework in place that serves individual as well as collective and systemic priorities. The institutionalized system of coaching teams and study groups assists individuals in learning and implementing new skills whether the initiative originated with individual interest, as a school-wide concern or a district-wide thrust. The Opal School faculty has learned to coordinate efforts in staff development and avoid the fragmentation that prevents effective learning in any area.

In training settings, they tend to request theory and demonstration in proportion to their needs, thus drawing from the instructor in any given situation the elements they know they will need for eventual skill mastery and implementation. They prefer opportunities to practice with feedback in the training setting but know they can provide practice and feedback to each other in the school setting if training time is limited. They are likely to draw from trainers references on the effectiveness of specific practices/skills/strategies and incorporate such reading into their study group sessions. Most important, they understand the requirements for transfer and have expedited the transfer process for themselves by organizing permanent structures that facilitate the mastery of theory, skills, and application.

SUMMARY

From the research on training and studies of transfer of training as well as clinical experience over the last 20 years, we have identified teacher skills, understandings and characteristics that appear to facilitate learning. The concern for identification of "learning-to-learn" skills stems from the contradictions that exist between skill learning and use of those skills in staff development programs. That teachers can learn a wide variety of skills, strategies and practices is well documented. That behaviors learned in training settings are less often implemented in classroom practice is also well documented, even though more intensive training programs that include follow-up training and employ peer self-help groups have much better implementation records than the field as a whole.

Snow (1982), commenting on three papers prepared for a symposium on "The Student's Role in Learning," notes that "learning is a function of the amount of active mental effort invested in the exercise of intelligence to accomplish cognitive work" (p. 5). He further asserts that "it is possible to train directly the cognitive and metacognitive processing skills involved in intelligent learning and it is possible to prompt intrinsically motivated learning by intelligent arrangement of educational conditions" (p. 10). If the skills and characteristics identified in this chapter do indeed help teachers learn from training opportunities to the extent that they are better able to master and implement new content and instructional practices, we are a step closer to developing the conditions that enable teachers to master the "cognitive and metacognitive processing skills involved in intelligent learning."

From a career perspective, it may be that learning how to acquire good practices should take a place of substantively equal importance with the good practices themselves. The effectiveness of preservice teacher training programs may well depend on the skill of the teacher candidates to navigate the consolidation phase in the variety of settings in which they will find themselves. The creation of effective inservice training programs may equally depend on the skills of teachers to learn ever increasing knowledge and practices and how to consolidate them. Current staff development efforts expend a large portion of their energy in persuasion and in helping teachers cope with anxiety and stress. The situation might be quite different if those same teachers had been adequately prepared for the life-long process of professional education.

CHAPTER SEVEN

THE COACHING
OF TEACHING

Imagine two highly enthusiastic teachers who are studying a model of teaching (for example, Synectics) in a series of workshops. In two three-day workshops they receive initial training and study the theory of synectics, see demonstrations, practice in peer teaching settings. Then they are to practice in their classrooms and, a month after the second initial workshop, come together again in the training setting to share experiences, see further demonstrations, and plan applications. At one-month intervals, three follow-up sessions are held, each one designed to support practice and probe more deeply into the model. They also are given videotapes to watch at their school site or at home.

One teacher, Martin, belongs to the study group in the Onyx school and is accompanied by a teammate. A second, Charles, is there on his own. Charles tried to recruit a companion but no one was interested in his school. The principal agreed to arrange for substitute time for him to attend the workshops but was somewhat grudging about it and expressed his hope that the emphasis on creativity would not detract from the basic curriculum.

After the first two workshops both Martin and Charles displayed a good level of skill in Synectics — enough to sustain practice in the opinion of the instructor and both were able to generate plans for using it in the teaching of writing and the social studies.

Back in their schools, each tried the model twice the first week. As their instructor had forewarned them, each found that the chief task in learning to use the model was in teaching it to the students. The students were awkward in the first trials and both teachers felt a bit discouraged, especially since they had found the approach to be enjoyable as well as useful. Martin and his coaching partner visited one another that week and, discussing the experience afterward, found themselves laughing about their common surprise. "We thought it would be easy the first time," summed up Martin's partner, "They were right when they said we'd have to teach the students how to participate." Over the next few weeks they set out to do exactly that. By the time the second workshop rolled around, each had practiced 10 times and were ready for an advanced session. They brought tapes to the workshop so the instructor could help them analyze their teaching and prepare for the next practices.

Charles, on the other hand, tried the model only once more before the second workshop, deciding to wait for more instruction before he continued to practice. He found that Martin and some of the others were far ahead of him and couldn't understand why he had not practiced more. He felt left out and confused and had trouble following some of the questions they were asking the instructor. Nonetheless he left the first follow-up workshop with renewed resolve. Back in the classroom he found that the students were as awkward as they had been at the beginning, but he persisted and tried the model a half-dozen more times before the second follow-up session, and made a good deal of progress.

Meantime, Martin and his partner had made the model a regular part of instruction in writing and social studies and were looking for new applications. At the second workshop Charles found himself in a group who, like him, were about at the stage Martin had been in after the first four weeks. He made an acquaintance whose principal agreed to free her to visit Charles' school so they could practice together with his classes. They did so, practicing twice each week. By the third follow-up session, they were dealing with the same issues that Martin and his partner were.

This story has a happy ending and in Hollywood all of them would join the training cadre and start to spread the good word to others.

In real life, many of us do not have the persistence Charles showed and even fewer find a coaching partner who can manage to get free to work with them even though they work in different schools.

Yet, for most of us, learning a new approach to teaching – a new piece of repertoire – will require 20 or 25 trials and the assistance of someone who can help us analyze the students' responses and enable us to stick with the process until we have executive control over our new skill.

Staff development programs can be conceived as serving three constituencies – individuals, schools, and districts. Individual teachers often request staff development offerings in their specific subject areas or in topics they feel will enhance their personal growth as teachers. Thus, teachers in a single school might request training in science, math, writing, classroom management, alternative teaching strategies, test development, and organizational development.   Generally, central office personnel poll teachers to determine their interests and arrange for a variety of offerings in response to those interests.

Staff development programs designed to support school-based initiatives are intended to serve entire faculties in their school improvement efforts. Thus, if a school adopted as its goal for a year the introduction of cooperative learning across subject areas and grade levels, training would aim to develop teacher competence in adapting cooperative learning strategies to their individual situations and administrator competence in organizing and facilitating cooperative learning structures.

System-wide initiatives usually attempt to introduce new knowledge or skills to all teachers in a district.   For example, a board may adopt a resolution introducing computer use at all grade levels and appropriate funds to buy hardware and software. Staff development to support such a systemic initiative would then provide appropriate training to all personnel, both in terms of their own familiarity with computers and in their ability to teach children to use computers.

The needs of the individual, school, and system all have legitimate claims on staff development resources.   Presently, however, many district staff development programs are over-invested, proportionately, in the individual rather than school or system-wide initiatives.   The preponderance of brief offerings on a large number of topics suggests that many people are being introduced to a multitude of concepts in a cursory fashion. We would argue that more staff development resources be committed to school-based initiatives in order to focus limited resources on collective efforts to implement change.

THE PURPOSES OF COACHING

In chapter six we discussed the design of training programs and the research on its effects.   In general, training is expected to result in sufficient skill that practice can be sustained in the classroom and transfer of new practices into the working repertoires of teachers.   Later in this chapter we will examine the warrant under the claim for coaching as a device for facilitating transfer of training.

While coaching programs can support the implementation of individual or system initiatives, its organization and institutionalization happen at the school level. **The major purpose of peer coaching programs is implementation of innovations to the extent that determination of effects on students is possible.**

Coaching has several other purposes.   One is to build communities of teachers who continuously engage in the study of their craft.   Coaching is as much a communal activity as it is the exercise of a set of skills and a vital component of training. Second, coaching develops the shared language and common understandings necessary for the collegial study of new knowledge and skills. Especially important is the agreement that curriculum and instruction need constant improvement and that expanding our repertoire of teaching skills requires hard work, in which the help of our colleagues is indispensable. Third, coaching provides a structure for the follow-up to training that is essential for acquiring new teaching skills and strategies. Researchers of teacher training (Joyce & Showers, 1983), curriculum implementation (Fullan & Pomfret, 1977), and curriculum reform (Shaver, Davis, & Helburn, 1978; Weiss, 1978) agree that transfer of skills and strategies foreign to the teacher's existing repertoire requires more substantial training than that typically allotted to such enterprises. Coaching appears to be most appropriate when teachers wish to acquire unique configurations of teaching patterns and to master strategies that require new ways of thinking about learning objectives and the processes by which students achieve them.

CHARACTERISTICS OF COACHING

Coaching programs are characterized by several conditions. First, they are **attached to training** programs. Coaching relationships continue and extend training in the workplace as trainees attempt to master and implement new knowledge, skills, and strategies.

Training content changes over time as people master, adapt, and use learned skills and then turn to new challenges. The community of learners engaged in the **continuous** study of teaching, curriculum, and academic content, however, is permanent. Coaching is a set of continuing relationships and structures for self-help that serves individual, school, and systemic initiatives for educational improvement. Membership in coaching teams may be fluid and organized around different objectives. Thus, an individual at one time may be a member of a coaching team comprised of individuals working on a specific teaching strategy in which all are personally interested. At another time this individual may be part of a grade-level team working on writing strategies as part of a school-wide effort to improve the quality of student writing. Later he or she may join a cross-department team working on instructional applications for computers in the classroom as part of a district-wide effort to increase general computer literacy.

Coaching is **experimental** in nature. Teachers in coaching teams not only work to master new skills learned in training settings but explore the most appropriate occasions for use of their new skills. Their search entails experimenting with learning objectives not usually included in their instructional plans, reorganizing existing curricular materials and creating new ones, working out classroom management strategies that facilitate different learning processes, and evaluating the effects of their experiments before redesigning the next efforts. This exploratory cycle continues until teachers are confident that they have achieved both technical mastery and appropriate use of new skills and strategies.

Because of the experimental nature of adapting new educational knowledge and practice to classroom settings, coaching relationships are completely **separate from supervision and evaluation** cycles. As we practice coaching, every aspect of the training process is carefully studied. Coaching teams measure their transfer of skills to the workplace and study the effectiveness of teaching skills and strategies with their students. In this sense, everything is evaluated. However, nothing could be farther from the atmosphere of coaching than is the practice of traditional evaluation. The norms of coaching and evaluation practice are antithetical and should be separated in our thinking as well as in practice. By definition, evaluation should not be undertaken concurrently with coaching, whereas the analysis of skills and their use is an inherent part of it.

After coaching has brought teachers to a level of transfer in which newly learned behaviors are skillfully and appropriately applied, teachers should study the effects on children as a means of improving performance. Teachers need sufficient time to learn and master new skills before they are evaluated on the adequacy of their performance of the new skills or the effects of those skills on student learning.

THE MECHANICS OF PEER COACHING

The actual organization of peer coaching programs is relatively simple — peer coaches need time to watch each other work and time to talk. Peer coaching assumes a common training experience, in which participants have learned not only new knowledge, skills, and strategies but also a common language regarding what they are attempting to implement and shared understandings about the purposes of their new practices. During training, participants study the rationale of new skills, see them demonstrated, practice them, and learn to provide feedback to one another as they experiment with the skills.

Following initial training, coaching is a cyclical process designed as an extension of training. The first steps are structured to increase skill through practice, observation, and feedback. These early sessions provide opportunities for checking performance against expert models of behavior. In our practice and study of coaching, teachers use Clinical Assessment Forms (Joyce & Showers, 1986) to record the presence or absence of specific behaviors and the degree of thoroughness with which they are performed.

Because all teachers learn to use the forms during initial training sessions and are provided practice by checking their own and each others' performance with these forms, they are prepared to provide feedback to each other during the coaching phase. Whether teachers are studying new models of teaching, implementing a new curriculum or exploring new technologies, feedback must be accurate, specific, and nonevaluative.

As skill develops and solidifies, coaching moves into a more complex stage – mutual examination of appropriate use of a new teaching strategy. The cognitive aspects of transferring new behaviors into effective classroom practice are more difficult than the interactive moves of teaching. While all teachers can develop skill in performing a new teaching strategy fairly readily, the harder tasks come as the skill is applied in the classroom. For example, when teachers master inductive teaching strategies, such as concept attainment and inductive thinking, they have little difficulty learning the pattern of the models and carrying them out with materials provided to them. However, many teachers have difficulty selecting concepts to teach, reorganizing materials, teaching their students to respond to the new strategies, and creating lessons in areas in which they have not seen specific demonstrations. Generally, these are the kinds of tasks that become the substance of coaching. Each model of teaching and each curriculum generate similar problems that must be solved if transfer to the classroom is to be achieved.

As the process shifts to this second set of emphases, coaching conferences take on the character of collaborative problem-solving sessions, which often conclude with joint planning of lessons the team will experiment with. Team members (note that all members are both coaches and students) begin to operate in a spirit of exploration. They search for and analyze curriculum materials for appropriate use of strategies, hypothesize student responses and learning outcomes for specific strategies, and design lessons. The "teacher" experiments with a new lesson while the "coach" observes, and the experimentation continues with a new cycle of analysis, study, hypothesis-forming, and testing.

The actual appearance of coaching programs varies widely from setting to setting. One elementary school faculty divided itself into three study groups, each with the intention of mastering a new teaching strategy and eventually teaching it to the rest of the faculty. Each third of the faculty was released for three days, respectively, until they had all completed initial training in a teaching strategy. Because teachers on this faculty had no "prep" periods, they did not observe each other teach on a weekly basis. Rather, their principal and administrative intern each taught one class a day, releasing two people to observe their coaching partners. Teachers videotaped their classroom trials and shared them in team meetings on a bi-weekly basis, while most of each monthly faculty meeting was devoted to analysis of taped or live lessons with children. Although each teacher had a peer coach, the coaching community actually functioned as teams of eight teachers studying a single model of teaching and as an entire faculty studying instructional strategies.

We have seen more than one high school district where teachers have simply used their preparation periods to observe each other teach or share videotapes of teaching. In some cases, entire departments have arranged to have the same preparation period during the school day in order to devote time once a week to the study of teaching and academic content. In one wealthy district, teachers were released by a substitute once a week in order to observe each other teach. In chapter eleven we will discuss cost-free ways of freeing time for the collaborative study of teaching. In general, we recommend against spending precious staff development dollars on released time for teachers in coaching programs and advocate the use of alternative means for securing the necessary time.

RESEARCH ON COACHING

Understanding of how education personnel can help each other has come from a variety of sources. Only within the last 15 years, however, have the processes of training and implementation come under close scrutiny. By the early 1970's it had become recognized that a great many efforts to improve schools, even when very well funded and approved by the public, had encountered great difficulty and achieved very low levels of implementation. Since that time, innovators, students of school organization, curriculum development personnel, and technologists concerned with such innovations as computers in the classroom have behaved much less naively. The nature of training, organizational climate, curriculum implementation, the processes by which teachers learn, and the organization of the school district itself have been attended to with much greater care. We draw on all of these for our knowledge about how all personnel can work together to ensure that skill development and the mastery of content result from training, and that personnel are skillful in the collaborative effort to transfer those products into active educational practice.

We acknowledge the work of many of our colleagues in the development of coaching programs for transfer of training. The concept of teachers as trainers has been explored by Bentzen (1974), Devaney and Thorn (1975), and Sharan and Hertz-Lazarowitz (1982), among others. Berman and McLaughlin (1975) noted the importance of in-class assistance and teachers observing other teachers for effective educational change programs. Fullan and Pomfret (1977) cited the importance of training and administrative support in the implementation of curriculums.

The work most similar to ours is that of Sharan and Hertz-Lazarowitz (1982). They provided extensive initial training (52 hours) to teachers learning a complex new teaching strategy and supported the initial training with consultant-assisted self-help teams composed of three or four teachers. The teams engaged in cooperative planning of teaching processes and content, mutual observation of teaching, and feedback by teammates to the teacher being observed. Their teacher self-help teams were developed on the basis of earlier work by Nelson (1971) and Roper, Deal, and Dornbusch (1976). In the second year of their project, 65 percent of the participating classroom teachers were using small group teaching (group investigation) regularly and appropriately.

As we studied the work of Sharan and his associates, we were struck by the thoroughness and duration of training, the consistency of in-class follow-up, and particularly by the help provided by peers to each other as they attempted to implement a teaching process quite different from their normal practice.

We can divide the results of our studies of coaching into two categories: facilitation of transfer of training and development of norms of collegiality and experimentation.

Coaching appears to contribute to transfer of training in five ways.

1. Coached teachers generally practice new strategies more frequently and develop greater skill in the actual moves of a new teaching strategy than do uncoached teachers who have experienced identical initial training (Showers, 1982). Apparently, the support and encouragement provided by peers while attempting new teaching strategies helps to sustain practice through the often awkward stages of implementing different teaching practices and teaching students how to respond to them. Even though uncoached teachers had shared 30 hours of training with coached teachers, they tended to practice the strategies little or not at all following training, despite their stated intentions to use the new models of teaching for classroom instruction.

2. In our studies, coached teachers used their newly learned strategies more appropriately than uncoached teachers in terms of their own instructional objectives and the theories of specific models of teaching (Showers, 1982; 1984). Coached teachers had opportunities to discuss with each other instructional objectives, the strategies that theoretically were best-designed to accomplish those objectives, and the types of curricular materials that would be needed for specific strategies. Consequently, they experimented with new instructional strategies in their own curriculum areas more quickly than uncoached teachers and shared lessons and materials with each other early in the coaching

process. Uncoached teachers, on the other hand, tended to practice in their classrooms using lessons they had seen as demonstrations or in peer practice during initial training sessions. Once they had exhausted those possibilities, they had difficulty finding appropriate occasions for use in their own curriculum areas and tended to quit practicing. Interestingly, however, regular interviews revealed their continuing intention to use the strategies as soon as they had time to think through their potential applications.

3. Coached teachers exhibited greater long-term retention of knowledge about and skill with strategies in which they had been coached and, as a group, increased the appropriateness of use of new teaching models over time (Baker & Showers, 1984). Six to nine months after training in several new models of teaching, coached teachers had retained, and in several instances, increased their technical mastery of the teaching strategies. Uncoached teachers, however, were in many cases unable to even demonstrate the new strategies after that period of time had elapsed. They were as surprised as we were by the loss of skill, although in retrospect we all should have realized that disuse over a spring, summer, and fall time period would lead to skill loss.

4. In our study of peer coaching (Showers, 1984), coached teachers were much more likely than uncoached teachers to teach new models of teaching to their students, ensuring that students understood the purpose of the strategy and the behaviors expected of them when using the strategy. For example, students of coached teachers were more likely to understand the nature and definition of concepts, metaphors, and analogies and were therefore more able to operate independently with concept attainment and synectics teaching strategies. These students not only had more experience (practice) with the strategies but had been provided direct instruction in component model skills. Students of uncoached teachers, on the other hand, had insufficient practice with the strategies to develop skill and confidence with them. Therefore, when their teachers occasionally attempted one of the new strategies, the more outspoken students were likely to suggest that they not waste time with the new strategy but rather conduct the lesson in ways with which they were all familiar and, by implication, competent.

5. Finally, coached teachers in our studies exhibited clearer cognitions with regard to the purposes and uses of the new strategies, as revealed through interviews, lesson plans, and classroom performance than did uncoached teachers (Showers, 1982; 1984). The frequent peer discussions regarding appropriate use of strategies, objectives for which specific models were more suited, experiments with use of strategies in ways different from those studied in training, design of lessons and

materials, etc. seemed to enable coached teachers to think with the new strategies in ways that the uncoached teachers never exhibited. Uncoached teachers who did occasionally use the trained models of teaching tended not to depart, at least consciously, from the exact forms and applications they had experienced in training. Therefore, if in training the synectics strategy was demonstrated as a pre-writing activity and organizer for writing, uncoached teachers were unlikely to apply synectics to problem-solving situations. Or, if an inquiry strategy was demonstrated with science content, uncoached teachers were less likely to apply the strategy to investigation of social policies or questions in anthropology and literature.

Coaching appears to facilitate the professional and collegial relationships discussed by Little (1982); for example, development of a shared language and norms of experimentation. Our data about this process are somewhat less formal than that on skill acquisition and transfer. However, both anecdotal and interview data indicate that the effects of coaching are much more far reaching than the mastery and integration of new knowledge and skills by individual teachers. The development of school norms that support the continuous study and improvement of teaching apparently build capability for other kinds of change, whether it is adoption of a new curriculum, a schoolwide discipline policy, or the building of teaching repertoire. By building permanent structures for collegial relationships, schools organize themselves for improvement in multiple areas. We suspect that the practice of public teaching; focus on the clinical acts of teaching; development of common language and understanding; and sharing of lesson plans, materials, and problems contribute to school norms of collegiality and experimentation. However, we don't know exactly how coaching programs function to create such norms or if existing norms create favorable climates for coaching programs.

COACHING AND THE ROLE OF OTHER EDUCATION PERSONNEL

As districts begin to include coaching as a part of their staff development programs, a variety of questions arise about coaching's relationship to roles played by principals and other education staff.

Coaching and the Principal

Establishing a coaching program requires strong leadership from school principals as well as support from central administrative staff. The leadership is manifested in priority-setting, resource allocation, and the logistics of scheduling on the one hand and substantive and social leadership on the other.

Administrators need to examine carefully their priorities for staff development and their allocation of funds. Few staff development budgets can sustain both intensive, ongoing training and the numerous one-shot activities that dominate most programs. Decisions must be made regarding the outcomes expected of a staff development program. When the desired outcome is simply increased awareness of a subject, funding might legitimately support the occasional two-hour speaker. However, when the expected outcome of staff development is change in the instruction students receive, funding probably will have to be focused to support the magnitude of training necessary to bring about that change.

Organization of peer-coaching systems will need to be arranged cooperatively between district administrators and school site personnel. In schools where teachers already have preparation periods scheduled into their work days, coaching teams can be organized for observation, feedback, and planning within existing structures. Creative problem solving by teachers and principals will result in solutions to the time demands of the continuous study and analysis of teaching. Without the active support and involvement of building principals, however, few teachers are able to establish such systems for themselves.

Principals must do more than assist with the logistics of peer-coaching systems if coaching is to become institutionalized. Teachers have worked so long in isolation that long-term collegial working relationships with their peers may be uncomfortable at first. Principals must work to establish new norms that reward collegial planning, public teaching, constructive feedback, and experimentation. Professional growth must be seen as valuable and expected. Where coaching has flourished, principals have taken very active roles in helping teams form, supporting them, providing times in meetings for sharing of teaching and planning, and providing help for team leaders.

Not only are principals in a unique position to influence building norms, they are also perfectly situated to facilitate the implementation of peer coaching systems through collaborative problem solving with their teachers. Principals can design flexible scheduling for training, observation, feedback, and planning to meet the needs of individual faculties; offer rewards and incentives to encourage developing norms of collegiality; and solicit support from parents and community members by explaining the purpose and expected outcomes of intensive training programs embedded in larger school improvement efforts.

COACHING AND SUPERVISORS

The relationship between coaching and supervision within a district depends on power and status differentials. The development of common languages for the study of teaching, the organization of inquiring teams, and the objective analysis of teaching are compatible with supervision. However, supervision in many districts maintains the imbalance of power by placing administrators and other nonteaching personnel in supervisory roles and by combining evaluation with supervision. Decision-making authority for the most part remains in the hands of the superiors, with teachers the recipients of the process.

Where there has been a failure to separate evaluation and the status and power differences from supervision, it is improbable that the process will create a climate conducive to learning and growing on the part of the teachers. Certainly it is possible to imagine climates where status relationships operate productively, but frequently they do not appear to do so in education. One example of counter-productivity in another area is the extremely hierarchical structure of the military, which tends to prevent promotion of the leadership attributes most needed in times of war. The initiative required in effective teaching is incompatible with hierarchical dependency relationships.

Alone, the power differential operating in supervision is insufficient to impede learning — most of us seek expert help when we attempt to master a new skill, such as skiing, cooking, or writing. It is more likely that the evaluative component of supervision prevents the very climate essential for learning, that of experimentation and permission to fail, revision and trying again while continuously practicing new but still awkward skills and procedures. When evaluation is the end product of supervision, those being evaluated will generally put their best foot forward, demonstrate only those well-tested procedures that have been perfected over long periods of use and with which both they and their students are completely familiar. Even if these procedures are patently flawed, they feel safer than attempting something new and experimental.

In divorcing itself from evaluation, coaching provides a safe environment in which to learn and perfect new teaching behaviors, experiment with variations of strategies, teach students new skills and expectations inherent in new strategies, and thoughtfully examine the results. By placing the major responsibility for coaching with peers, status and power differentials are minimized. Of course, coaching draws on many of the elements of better supervisory programs — observation, feedback, cooperative planning, extended time frames. However, the elimination of evaluation and power inequities makes possible a learning environment that is unlikely in traditional supervisory systems. Furthermore, coaching has the added practical advantage of a wide-scale implementation for lengthy periods of time. Even exceptionally conscientious principals with superb interpersonal staff relationships have difficulty providing clinical supervision to more than a fraction of their teachers on a continuing basis.

IMPLEMENTING COACHING PROGRAMS

To be implemented successfully, coaching must overcome some obstacles. The social changes required by coaching in the workplace represent a major departure from the traditional school organization. The building of collegial teams that study teaching on a continuing basis forces the restructuring of administrative and supervisory staff. If the norms of the learning laboratory are to be established, a scientific rather than hierarchical spirit must prevail. Implementation of coaching requires an increase in objective feedback and evaluation of process and a reduction of judgmental pronouncements about teaching. A coaching system builds a community of teachers that inquires into teaching with the assistance of support personnel rather than teachers who work as isolated individuals and are judged by supervisors and administrators who visit and observe.

Coaching is inseparable from an intensive training program. The serious and continuing study of teaching in schools requires challenging substance, for which theory is thoroughly explicated and understood, demonstrations are provided, and opportunities for practice with feedback allow development of skill as well as knowledge. Without fully elaborated training programs, coaching has nothing upon which to build. Whenever districts ask us to help them design coaching programs, we first examine their training programs for both content and process.

Furthermore, support systems in many districts must be remolded to permit the meeting of collegial teams for study, observations, feedback, discussion, and planning. And the activities of coaching teams must be encouraged and supported by norms, rewards, and incentives in the school structure. The invaluable role of principals in facilitating coaching programs cannot be emphasized too strongly.

The cooperation between central office administrators and building principals can be seen most clearly in the development of cadres of teachers and supervisors who are organized to deliver training. The cadres have to be selected, freed to receive and later to give training, and given access to teams within the schools to engage in training and to help the teams develop. Without such cadres of trainers and the change of relationship that occurs when teachers and supervisors work together as trainers, coaching cannot be implemented.

SUMMARY

At this stage, coaching is an innovation, subject to the same laws that govern any other change in an educational setting. It is also a community of learners engaged in the study of teaching, a set of technical moves embodied in training and follow-up to that training, and a support system that creates and sustains the learning community and enables it to function. Hence, coaching is not a simple additive that can be tacked on with a business as usual attitude, but rather represents a change in the conduct of business. Some of these changes are social and some are technical. On the surface it should be simple to implement — what could be more natural than teams of professional teachers working on content and skills with the facilitation of building principals and administrators? It is a complex innovation only because that scene requires a radical change in relationships between teachers and between teachers and administrative personnel.

The coaching relationship is simply a partnership in which two or more people work together to achieve a goal. Visiting one another as they practice, they learn from observing the other person and particularly by watching the students' responses to the cognitive and social tasks that are presented to them. They discuss how to help the students respond more powerfully and how and where to apply their new skills.

We have many people who believe that the essence of the coaching transaction is in the offering of advice to the partner who is observed. It is not. Each partner learns by *watching* the transaction. Each teaches by *demonstration* rather than by criticizing the other person's behavior. Hence a partnership is forged in the continuing career-long experiment on how to teach more effectively.

CHAPTER EIGHT

THE NATURE OF THE SKILLS UNDERLYING GOOD PRACTICE

Throughout this book we have emphasized that a major purpose of human resource development systems in education is to encourage, and even ensure, that good practices are used in the instructional setting, which at this time in education is the classroom. We have also stressed that there is a large reservoir of good practices that are not used currently in most classrooms and that many practices that are common could be used more strongly or appropriately. We have described training research that indicates that most teachers (nearly all) have the capability to learn a large variety of new teaching strategies and to improve the ones in their existing personal storehouses, provided appropriate training strategies are combined.

We now turn to a brief consideration of the dynamics of the skills that permit the best practices to be used regularly. In the nature of these skills lie the reasons why the effective training pattern, the Theory-Demonstration-Practice-Feedback combination, when it is well-implemented, allows most teachers to learn even the very complex skills that enable them to use the powerful models of teaching, and why practice with companionship (the Coaching component) is necessary for those skills to be adapted and incorporated into the active repertoire of teachers.

"Skill" is used with a variety of denotive and connotive meanings in both colloquial and professional contexts. Even dictionary definitions, while less varied than colloquial meanings, illustrate the variety. The New Webster Dictionary (New Webster's, 1981) emphasizes that skill is not simply the ordinary production of behavior. For the authors of that dictionary, special training or attention is required. The New Oxford Illustrated Dictionary (New Oxford, 1978) emphasizes expertness, also including the component of training or practice. The assumption is that ordinary life experience does not produce the skill unless accompanied by special practice or training. The Collins Standard Dictionary (Collins, 1978) lays stress on greatness of ability. A behavior that anyone could do would not be labelled a skill. Webster's New Collegiate dictionary emphasizes both that the behavior must be practiced and used appropriately for an end, including the intentional application of knowledge; "the ability to use one's knowledge effectively and readily in execution of performance; . . . learned power of doing something competently: a developed aptitude or ability."

As we have studied the research, we have been impressed with the variety of behaviors that have been identified as skill, and the distinction between ordinary behavior and behavior that needs training not generally provided to most people.

We feel that professional skills may either be the production of ordinary behavior that is guided by knowledge that requires special education or extraordinary behavior, which most people would not develop without training or specific education.

SOME CONSIDERATIONS ABOUT SKILL

As we examine the research on teaching a number of considerations emerge that help us understand the enigmatic nature of teaching skills.

- *Intentionality backed up by knowledge.* All the yield from research shares the attribute of intentionality--doing something because it is believed that it will make a difference. Professional skill involves more than doing something because it is customary or feels right. Customs and intuitions may work, but they are not based on shared and examined professional knowledge.
- *Ordinariness/expertness.* In some cases it is the intentional production of an ordinary behavior that produces results, with no implication that the behavior need be developed through arduous practice. The giving of homework is an example. By increasing practice, it has effect. Expertness in the giving of homework so that there is enthusiastic, motivated, and directed attention to the tasks is less ordinary, although still hardly exotic. However, regulating homework because of knowledge about the nature of practice and feedback and how to mix those productively with demonstrations and other kinds of instruction, elevates the ordinary behavior into the expert realm.

Other skills, such as the management of cooperative inquiry in the classroom, are manifested by very few teachers without substantial amounts of training and/or practice, and thus can be classified as "expert" both because the skills and the knowledge to guide them require special training.

• *Environment and learner.* The effect of teaching is on learning. It is the effort of the learner that produces the learning. From a measurement perspective we can see this in the percent of variance in learning, frequently more than 75 percent, that is attributable to learner characteristics. Dewey's (1916, 1937) formulation that learning is the product of the interaction of the learner with the environment continues to be useful as we try to come to grips with the nature of teaching skill. The teacher can create aspects of the environment. The learner interacts with the environment. The relationship between the skill that creates the environment and the actual learning that takes place will have to be expressed in probabilistic terms. This is more than a matter of individual differences in reaction to environments. It is a matter of the nature of the relationship between the teacher and the learner. Teachers can use skills to affect the environment with the expectation that they have affected the probability that the learner will be activated and that learning will take place. This creates interesting problems for the research worker who must ferret out the nature of the relationships and an equally interesting problem for the practitioner who would understand and use the results. The language with which research findings are expressed and received must be constructed carefully. If either researcher or consumer use the language that would be appropriate for skills in hammering (if you strike the nail with a given force, a predictable effect will be achieved), the one will give the wrong impression and the other will be disappointed.

• *Context.* Teaching also takes place in a variety of contexts, and setting may alter the contribution of skills to learning. What works very well in a tutorial center in a resource-based instructional system may not contribute much in a typical classroom setting. Also, wherever technology is an aspect of the educational environment, the designers and producers of the technology may also be teachers and their skills may interact with those of the on-site training agent and alter the impact of skills. Even within the same setting skills may be transformed by the use of different instructional modes. What works in a discussion (M. Gall & J. Gall, 1976) may not facilitate learning in a lecture or tutorial.

The criterion by which we judge a skill can be altered by changes in the setting. Concrete illustrations abound in sports. Imagine, for example, a basketball player who has learned to produce a jump shot in a gymnasium. He or she can dribble, turn, jump, and shoot and can make three-fourths of his or her shots from 15 feet. Now we alter the setting by introducing an opponent. The player can no longer move unimpeded but must learn to evade and fake. Those skills, to be effective, must be deceptive, however elegant they may appear. To further complicate the problem, we can introduce the rest of the two teams. Our player's jump shot now is embedded in a matrix of skills that other players must have as well. In the worst circumstances, we may not get to see the jump shot at all. The skill remains, but only as a potential. The analogy is not inappropriate to teaching. And, like sports, certain skills may only be effective if they can be modulated to fit circumstances – the shifting scene of students, group dynamics, materials, and other aspects of the environment. Skills may have to be learned as adaptable, with principles for modulation built into them and exercised regularly.

• *Observable and invisible skills.* In colloquial use, the term "skill" initially conjures up images of physical activity. Not unlike laymen, many educational researchers have concentrated on the observable acts of teaching. Increasingly, however, the mental and emotional components of skill are receiving attention. Some behaviors may be effective when they are produced routinely. Others may require considerable thought beforehand or intensive thought in the act of production. At one extreme, Schwab (1965) suggested that to be a fully effective biology teacher, one must engage continually in at least informal research in the field. Otherwise one loses touch with the process itself, the communication of which lies at the heart of scientific inquiry. To produce a behavior appropriately, or in some cases to produce it at all, may depend on substantial mental activities that constitute the invisible skills of teaching.

All of these considerations are important. At this point our stance is that good practices are permitted by skills that are directed toward an end, which have effect by creating environments that increase the probability that certain kinds of learning outcomes will ensue. These outcomes may be the careful direction of ordinary behavior but may require special training and surely must be modulated to their contexts, the students, and the settings where they will be used.

We have also become convinced that the overt, visible skills are driven by mental activities that constitute the invisible skills of teaching and that it is in understanding this intellectual dimension of teaching that we will learn why certain kinds of training produce the effects they do.

In this chapter we will draw on the analysis of skills needed to use a number of models of teaching. The large variety of overt skills that enable teachers to create the structure of the environments specified by theorists of curriculum and teaching have been studied and classifications offered in previous papers (Joyce, Showers, Beaton, & Dalton 1984, 1985). The current focus is on the nature of these skills and draws on studies of teachers and trainers as they carry out these models of teaching and enable others to use them, studies of teachers' thinking as they widen their repertoire of teaching models (Dalton & Dodd, 1986) and studies of teachers' needs as manifested during coaching sessions.

In the absence of training, nearly all teachers employ what is termed the "recitation" pattern of teaching as their primary approach. The recitation begins with instruction of some kind—from lectures, demonstrations, reading, seeing films, etc.—followed by practice and then a recitation, or demonstration, of what has been learned. In fact, the naturalistic studies of teaching indicate that a good many teachers use a rather limited version of recitation (Brophy & Good, 1986; Stallings, Needels, & Stayrook, 1979). Frequently what Good and his associates (1983) call "development" or the explanation/demonstration component of the recitation pattern is truncated or even left out altogether, leaving the students to practice or answer questions after a very limited amount of instruction. The prevalence of the recitation has two important implications. First, whenever a model of teaching is used as the substance of a staff development program, nearly all of the teachers in the study or program need to learn interactive and cognitive skills that are different from the ones to which they are accustomed. Second, each time we prepare teachers to use a teaching strategy new to them, we have the opportunity to watch them acquire new interactive skills and information-processing patterns or at least reassemble familiar skills into new patterns. For most practitioners, learning a theory-driven model is learning to use a tool other than the dominant recitation. For teachers who generally use what we call the "truncated" recitation, that is, those who leave out the "development" or instructional activity, a model that asks for presentation or demonstration asks them not only to teach differently, but to engage in a phase of teaching with which they have relatively little experience. Since nearly all preservice candidates either use the recitation spontaneously or are quickly socialized into it, their problems in learning a new model are parallel with, although not identical to the ones encountered by experienced teachers (Joyce, Peck, & Brown, 1981).

Preservice candidates can easily master a wide repertoire of teaching skills and the knowledge to use them effectively but in most teacher education programs the influence of cooperating teachers "pulls" them toward the recitation.

THE COGNITIVE AND INTERACTIVE DIMENSIONS OF TEACHING SKILL

Since Philip Jackson's and Nate Gage's very important 1966 papers and the 1974 conference on teaching that Gage organized for NIE it has been generally recognized that teaching can be thought of in terms of the preactive (planning) phase and the interactive episodes that have a cognitive or information-processing dimension as well as the visible behaviors of interaction.

From studies of normative practice it appears that most teaching episodes are planned rapidly (Clark & Yinger, 1979), that the student instructional materials are the chief sources consulted (Joyce & Harootunian 1967; Clark & Yinger, 1979), and that the interactive information processing (the thinking by teachers during the course of teaching) generally follows the pattern of the recitation with very few decisions that significantly alter the course of activities. Most decisions modify activities that have been established (McNair 1978-1979; Clark & Peterson, 1986; Peterson & Clark, 1978; Peterson, Marx, & Clark, 1978). Prepackaged instructional materials mesh nicely with the recitation and share its dominance in most classrooms. That teachers follow those materials closely is one reason why the preactive phase can be and is usually so brief. One can glance over the next chapter, take a peek at the workbook, and follow the pattern of activities that was established during the first few weeks of school. The materials are designed for self-study (seat work) and rarely are designed on an instructional model or as support for one. There is liberal review and the amount of new substance is relatively modest. The modesty of the pace is significant. For example, in one of Showers' current studies she discovered that one eighth grade literature course stretched the time for reading a 100-page written-for-adolescents novel to 15 days. The students were not allowed to take the books home (lest they read ahead). The novel was read silently or aloud in class followed by teacher questioning over what had been read. Recall-level questions dominated at a 10-1 ratio over open-ended queries or questions designed to induce concept formation or synthesis. Such a slow pace of substance followed essentially by only a factual review of what had been read does not require extensive planning.

The most common interactive moves in most classrooms include: the giving of directions (about 20 percent), asking and answering information-level questions (about 60 percent when the class is working as a whole, which is the norm), and positive sanctions and corrective feedback (about 10 percent). These are the most practiced moves for most teachers who use the recitation. (Obviously these are global descriptions and can be analyzed into a great variety and combination of behaviors.)

As we try to understand the nature of what teachers have to learn to implement a new teaching strategy or model we find information from observing them try to understand the theory of the model, by studying their behavior during the preactive phase of preparation for teaching episodes, and by observing them as they practice the interactive behaviors necessary to apply the model.

The Learning of Theory

Most of the illustrations in this chapter are of the skills required to employ three models of teaching. We have selected these because they are quite different from one another although there are certain educational goals that they can be directed toward in common. One is scientific inquiry, the inductive-oriented model developed from the methodology of the social and natural sciences. The second is the advance organizer model, developed from David Ausubel's (1963) theory of verbal learning. The third is group investigation, the democratic-process model revised and renovated by Herbert Thelen (1960) and currently studied by Shlomo Sharan. Each of the three models has a complex rationale that has to be mastered if preactive or interactive behaviors are to follow the model. In planning and execution the theory is a constant referent for the shaping of activities. This is one of the first aspects of cognitive skill that characterizes the theory-driven models. Mastery of the theory includes an understanding of its rationale (why its originators believe it will work), the conceptualization of its structure or syntax, the principles that guide reaction to student behavior, the nature of the social system it creates in the classroom, and the structure of the instructional materials that will support it. For teachers accustomed to the recitation the operational mastery of the theory of a model can be difficult. To use the theory effectively they not only have to grasp its essence but also learn how to arrange instructional materials and design interactive patterns so that the theory can operate. Until the theory can be visualized by teachers in concrete operational terms it is little good to them. We have found that many teachers display much anxiety in training sessions until that level of understanding is achieved. Most, but not all, need a very specific level of understanding. A large number of "What do you do if...?" Questions are asked. We hypothesize that they wish to visualize teaching episodes designed around the new (to them) theory in concrete terms that simulate the predictable sequence of the recitation. As a practical matter we mix demonstrations and practice with the study of theory when we design training. Despite this, many teachers have trouble imagining what will happen when they make initiatives in their own classroom that differ from the familiar moves of the recitation. A few years ago we were laboring with a group of teachers who seemed tremendously concerned with how children would respond to a move asking them to categorize information in inductive encounters. Observers had been in their classrooms for about four months at the time of the training workshop, but we had not seen summarized data to that point. It happened that right after a particularly laborious session the observers handed us a summary. Looking at it that evening, we discovered that 60 percent of the teachers had not asked a higher order question or stated a concept during any of the periods of observation! We concluded that they simply could not imagine how their children would respond to a task requiring conceptual activity. Small wonder that they were concerned with a level of detail we had taken for granted. Or that they were anxious about approaching a theory which, once operationalized, asks them to conduct teaching episodes where as much as 50 percent of the interaction will be at the conceptual level.

The operationalization of the theory requires the belief that the students can respond appropriately to the environment that will be created. Not unreasonably, teachers judge the competence of the students from the behaviors they are accustomed to observing. Without having previously observed responses to cognitive tasks of many kinds, a fair proportion of teachers simply have no evidence from which to estimate how the students will respond. Perhaps this is why so many teachers overestimate the ability of students they see during demonstrations of models that utilize complex cognitive and social tasks. Recently we made a series of videotapes of children from India engaged in a series of complex models. Aside from the confrontation with their stereotypes of Indian children (who are these well-dressed, well-spoken, inquisitive children?), almost uniformly teachers wonder if these students have not been culled from some elite population. Even when one demonstrates with the children from the schools in which they teach, there is a tendency for many teachers to believe that the results are probably a one-time aberration, a momentary burst of brilliance, and that the children probably will not behave like that again.

The mastery of the theory takes on great importance during the practice periods when teachers are using their new model in the classroom. A large number of the questions they ask during coaching sessions have to do with the nature and details of the theory. As they watch the children behave in unfamiliar ways they want to know why and what are the implications (Showers, 1982, 1984).

Designing Lessons: The Preactive Phase

Designing teaching episodes involves planning the activities, formulating the interactive moves that will guide them, and the assembly or adaptation of instructional materials. The structure of the model (what we generally refer to as its syntax) provides guidelines to the teacher. As they try to apply the syntax and guidelines for assembling the instructional materials in the planning process they can see the developing skill in operation. The advance organizer model provides a good example because the majority of its skills are exercised in the preactive phase. The actual delivery of advance organizers is not complex in itself and does not call for the development of unusual skills. It is in the formulation of the organizers that energy is consumed. The teacher must think through the material that is to be dealt with and develop or select the more powerful ideas for conceptualizing it. To help teachers do this we generally teach them to perform an inductive exercise over the material, developing concepts that can serve as organizers. We have the teachers arrange the concepts in little hierarchies that conform to Ausubel's theory. It becomes apparent that many of them have not regularly approached the content that they teach from a conceptual point of view. (Some have, of course.) Even when classifying such familiar material as the multiplication facts most teachers discover relationships that they have not detected previously, although they may have been teaching specific number facts for years. Similarly, when we provide conceptual frameworks from the disciplines, we discover that these are also new to most teachers. Whether they are asked to build conceptual frameworks or to use prepared ones, we find that many teachers have to learn to approach material conceptually as a general proposition.

Teachers who are habitual conceptualizers have a much easier time approaching all the information-processing models. Some years ago we learned that integrative complexity (Harvey, Hunt, & Schroeder, 1961) facilitates the acquisition of an expanded teaching repertoire (Joyce, Peck, & Brown, 1981) and is associated with the spontaneous use of complex social and cognitive tasks in the classroom (Hunt & Joyce, 1967). We believe that what we are seeing now in the response to training is consistent with those findings.

As instruction proceeds, some beliefs that accompany the recitation surface and cause interesting problems. Many teachers believe that retention is maximized if information is learned in isolated segments. Those persons tell us that conceptual approaches to teaching will probably reduce retention! They express the opinion that even the act of delivering an organizer will probably waste valuable class time. It is interesting that this response occurs during instruction in didactic models, such as the advance organizer, as well as the inductive and problem-solving ones. We think that there are several possible explanations for the concern that conceptual approaches to teaching will waste time. First, the recitation focuses largely on specific bits of information and is accompanied by an implicitly atomistic view of knowledge and a belief that learning is facilitated by a concentration on one atom at a time. Second, most tests focus on specific bits of information, a statement that they are important outcomes, perhaps the crucial ones, and provide a model for the teaching interchange. If the test is going to ask "How many legs has the fly?", it is an invitation to conduct instruction in a corollary fashion at the very least. Third, Pressley, Levin, and Delaney (1982) have demonstrated that nearly all of us usually try to acquire information through rote repetition. It is not unreasonable to theorize that most teachers themselves attack tasks requiring memorization by using rote strategies. Since we are likely to teach students to attack problems in the fashion that we do, our practice can provide implicit personal theory to apply in our teaching. Whatever the explanation, the belief can be strongly held and cannot be dealt with as if it were of no consequence.

If we are correct that the long experience with the recitation socializes many teachers to an atomistic theory of knowledge, to a belief that knowledge exists in isolated bits and is best learned bit by bit, then learning to think with the theories of almost all theory-based models requires the serious reexamination of the nature of knowledge and how it is acquired.

An Experimental Frame of Reference

Because learning alternative approaches to teaching requires many teachers to learn how students respond to unfamiliar tasks, in order to practice concept-oriented models with any gusto, teachers have to be willing to test the tasks prescribed by the theories. This need leads to another cluster of skills--the ability to conduct informal experiments in the classroom, giving students cognitive and social tasks and observing their behavior. In addition, the appropriate use of the model has to be faced (when do I work inductively, etc.?).

As indicated earlier, teachers who have had little experience in the use of complex social and intellectual tasks have little basis for predicting how the students will respond. They simply do not have any idea what students will do when they are asked to form concepts and many manifest great surprise when they learn that students not only can form concepts but, given time and appropriate material, can discover important concepts from the disciplines.

Instructional Materials

Then, appropriate materials have to be found or constructed. The inductive model provides a good illustration. It requires materials that can be categorized. Imagine a secondary social studies teacher whose courses are structured by narrative textbooks over which the recitation is conducted. In Schwab's terms (1982), the data presented by those textbooks is largely a "rhetoric of conclusions." The textbook names wars and generals and explains why those wars started and how international relations are conducted and when labor movements started. What first becomes apparent is that the materials of instruction that are most often used in American classrooms, taken lesson by lesson, provide very little material that is amenable to categorization. The teacher has to scan the structure of the course, looking for places where in-depth, inductive exercises might improve things. That is not easy for folks unaccustomed to doing it, and can increase planning time exponentially. Then, once some possible applications have been identified, appropriate material has to be found. Most persons need a course in instructional materials. They also need many demonstrations using a variety of materials and have a tendency to mimic those demonstrations. (If we use pictures as sources of data, the majority of teachers will use pictures.) The extent of literal imitation was illustrated during one of our recent workshops with secondary social studies teachers. We illustrated the use of original sources with some pages from Indian newspapers containing articles on events leading up to the assassination of Mrs. Gandhi. When we were done, a teacher of an advanced placement government course asked, "How am I going to get papers printed when the constitution was written?" He did not spontaneously recognize that the Constitution itself is an original document, or that the Federalist papers or quite a number of other sources lying close at hand might serve as information sources for his students.

Another interference from the recitation occurs at the point of the assembly of materials. It represents a rule-oriented structure. Using the textbook and its accompanying tests involves following some fairly clear, if sometimes implicit rules. Creating or identifying other materials involves confidence that one is applying more heuristic rules in a reasonable fashion. Most teachers need much practice, success, and approval to navigate the experiential road to competence.

Thus we can see that the tasks involved in the preactive phase of many models have a way of giving birth to needs for a complex of skills and knowledge. Also, until those skills become consolidated the preactive time will be much increased over what it usually is with the recitation. As competence increases, preparation time will fall. Highly skilled teachers have well-developed mental routines for planning (Dalton, 1986) that enable them to operate briskly over a range of instructional models.

The Interactive Dimension of Teaching: The Visible and Invisible Skills

Educational environments are created largely by posing cognitive and social tasks and teaching students to respond appropriately to them. In nearly all cases the theory-driven models result in cognitive and social activities and interaction patterns that are more complex than those of the recitation, complicating matters for the teacher. A further complication is that, during the early stages of use, the students have to learn sets of new behaviors, so teachers who are learning a new model have the added burden of doing so with inexperienced students who they have to teach to respond appropriately. To further build stress, the more complex tasks have less predictable consequences than does the recitation. In inductive models, students can generate all sorts of ideas, have to resolve differences, and may work the substance in ways the teacher cannot anticipate. The stress can be seen in the responses to stimulated recall prompts when teachers are engaged in their early trials (Dalton, 1986). After presenting data to students and asking students to group the data, teachers first practicing the inductive model and prompted to report what they were thinking when they initiated the categorizing activity, often say, "I sure hope they come up with the concept I have in mind." With experience, they come to learn what to expect and also how to deal with the unexpected. The manifestations of stress are consequently reduced. Their estimates of their competence are interesting to observe. Throughout stimulated-recall interviews, feedback sessions, and in conversation, many teachers display great dissatisfaction with themselves during the early trials. They appear to wish perfection right from the start and can be very hard on themselves. As much as we explain that they will need many trials and although they are in the company of other novices with the model who are struggling at the same level, they display disgust if anything does not go well. They need to learn a more detached perspective in order to avoid excessively unrealistic expectations for either themselves or the children. We believe that the recitation is again in evidence. The predictable patterns of the recitation and its clear rules and sense of order make it possible to teach with great smoothness. Leading immature students through cooperative inquiry is not smooth or predictable. We believe that one of the reasons people domesticate a model into the recitation is this search for smoothness and predictability. We watched an Indian teacher use a concept formation exercise for the first time with young children. She had placed a large number of geometric shapes on a feltboard. Then she held up a triangle and asked the students to identify other objects that could be grouped with it. She rejected some suggestions, including ones of four-sided figures that shared an angle with her triangle. As soon as someone suggested a triangle, she smiled, said, "good," and scooped all the other triangles from the board, saying, "and all these go with it too, don't they?" She is not unusual in seeking a way to reduce the ambiguity and pull the pattern of the lesson as close as possible toward the recitation.

Thus, in addition to learning to present the cognitive and social tasks to the students and teaching them how to respond, teachers need to learn to read the student responses to the tasks and observe themselves objectively as they work toward competence. In many ways the principles of reaction in a model – the guidelines for responding and reacting to students, are much more difficult for teachers to learn than are the moves that induce students to work through the structure of the model. Learning the reactive skills is further complicated because some students, in addition to having to learn to respond appropriately, make moves that try to coopt the teacher back toward the recitation. Some are not above using the same type of guilt-producing moves they make on their parents, only the referent being different. ("Why do you confuse us this way when you could just tell us the answer?" Reminiscent, of course, of "why do I have to get a job when you could just give me a car?") As Thelan (1960) pointed out so clearly nearly 25 years ago, the recitation provides a very comfortable and undemanding environment. Students can resist challenging tasks and can very easily make teachers feel guilty if challenge produces any sign of discomfort.

Thus, teachers need to learn to read the student moves, respond to improve their skills, resist cooptation, and all this requires the invisible skills of the interactive phase. We currently think of the cognitive skills of the interactive phase as syntax-related and reaction-related. The syntax-related cognitions accompany the initiation of various types of activity and the acquisition of the judgment to make timely moves. The reaction-related moves are those requiring rapid information-processing – the reading of "in-flight" information from the students and the construction of responses to student behavior (and, very important, the ability to withhold or delay responses). Judgment and internal control are very important. In the case of the syntax-related moves one needs to acquire a sense of when, how, and what is enough. The criteria for each model are different. Group investigation provides a good illustration, because its phases have the least concrete transitions. In the first phase the students are confronted with a puzzling situation or problem and asked to share their reactions to it. To move to the next phase we have to ask, "Has the problem been fully explored? Have a rich variety of reactions been made? Is everyone's opinion now represented?" And so on. Too early closure will stunt the rest of the inquiry; excessive exploration will stunt the development of synergy. Later, as students set hypotheses and get ready to collect relevant data, the teacher must ask, "Are the hypotheses good enough to sustain the inquiry? Are they clear to everyone? Are plans appropriate and does everyone understand them?"

Although we can explain these skills and demonstrate them through the use of stimulated recall to explore the thinking process of the demonstrator, the subtle and powerful dimensions of the skill to make these judgments requires practice. It is analogous to learning how hard to throw a ball to get it a certain distance. One could be presented with a mathematical equation involving force, trajectory, and the weight of the ball and explain the relationships, but the thrower has to practice to get the feel of the concept and be able to act on it. After some overthrows and underthrows, the skill begins to develop. When learning to use a new teaching strategy, at first the teachers acquire some moves that will enable them to move the syntax and initiate new activities. However, they have trouble reading the responses of the students and deciding how well they did. Most, in the absence of evidence, judge that they are doing poorly! With practice and observation, they develop the ability to read the student responses and make more objective judgments. Cognitions become less self-absorbed and they concentrate more on those judgments and begin to experiment with more ways of initiating phases of the model and observe their effects on the students. Then, they begin to learn to tune the activities by responding to information they gain from the student responses. If it turns out that hypotheses have not been well-formulated, for example, they ask the students to reflect on their quality and try to improve them. (In the earlier trials the teachers often have to muddle along with what the students produce initially.)

The reaction-related cognitions are very complex in comparison to the recitation. For example, one of the trickier parts of group investigation is that it requires consensus about certain aspects of process (what the group will do next) but not about opinions or which hypotheses to entertain. When a student moves to force closure on substance and prematurely eliminate competing ideas, the teacher has to process information rapidly and come to a decision about whether to interfere to keep things open a little longer and, if so, how to move so as to protect the student's ego and not stymie the process. Restraint is important. In the recitation, many teachers respond or react to nearly everything said by any student. They also ask questions that put people on the spot, but, hopefully are not damaging because the implicit rules of the recitation legitimatize and explain their behavior. Group investigation involves cooperative student activity facilitated by the teacher; to respond at the rate of the recitation would subvert the process. What is special about learning to control one's basis for reaction is the rapidity of interchanges. If a student asks "Why did Mr. Duvalier leave Haiti?" most teachers have trained themselves to respond immediately with an opinion. In a stimulated-recall interview where the recitation has been used, teachers will often say, if one queries what was in their mind when they answered a question, "Nothing?" Or, looking at the investigator as if at the deranged, "that's my job." Learning a new approach surfaces cognitions and makes them more complex. First of all, during the initial practices many of the opportunities simply whiz by unnoticed or before a response can be formulated. Stopping the tape at a student comment, we ask the teacher what thoughts were conscious and get the response, "That's the first time I realized she said that." With a little more practice the response becomes, "that was a real interesting comment. I couldn't figure out what to do, so I did nothing." Later that evolves to "I was looking to see if the other students had heard her. If they hadn't I was trying to decide what to do." Gradually, with practice, most teachers begin to use the theory of the model as a conscious guide to their reactions and develop better and better judgment about how to modulate their behavior. There has been an evolution from an automatic response to a series of rapid-fire thoughts involving subtle decision making.

SUMMARY

A few years ago we speculated that most teachers' information-processing became quite routine as they settled into the patterns of activities that would fill the year, and would provide the patterns for the days and hours. We also speculated that the patterns of thought for most teachers are intertwined with the materials-based recitation, and would become quite different if they were to use different patterns of teaching (Joyce, 1978-79). We also speculated that the visible, interactive skills needed to use the theory-driven models would be fairly easy for most teachers to produce if they could be done without thinking. Fortunately they cannot. And it appears to us that the really difficult, and interesting, skills of the theory-driven models are cognitive, both in the preactive and interactive phase.

The message for us as trainers is self-evident. Although superficially it might appear that demonstration and practice sessions focus on the visible interactive behaviors, effective training requires that they be suffused with attention to the invisible, cognitive skills that make it possible to operationalize the theory-driven models skillfully and effectively. The addition of stimulated-recall techniques to training, both in demonstrations and practice sessions, may turn out to be useful by providing an opportunity for explicit attention to the cognitive dimension of the skills.

The apparent problems caused by the socialization to the recitation pose interesting problems for teacher education. If the ability to translate research into practice is to be a major objective of teacher education, it may be that programs have to be structured to teach candidates how to learn teaching strategies, in contrast to the socialization into the recitation that characterizes most teacher education programs. The apparent development of an atomistic conception of knowledge is particularly disturbing, especially if it is in fact related to the socialization to the recitation.

Nevertheless, an affirmative message is the capability of teachers to learn widened repertoires of teaching strategies, provided appropriate training is available and they receive the support through practice to enable them to develop the cognitions that accompany smooth and powerful performance. For most teachers, about 20 to 25 practice sessions appear to be necessary to bring about the necessary adjustments. Generally speaking, it seems easier if those occur as close to the training sessions as possible. Hence, if three or four days of training is presented on what is for the participants a new model of teaching, and if they then practice about ten times during the next four to six weeks, have a follow-up session of more demonstrations and discussions of application, practice about 10 more times and have another follow-up session, most will be on their way and able to sustain practice by themselves.

CHAPTER NINE

EVALUATING STAFF DEVELOPMENT PROGRAMS

The purpose of evaluation is to provide information that can be used to improve the operation of the system and its components and to assess their effects. Designing the evaluation of staff development programs is difficult for a number of reasons. First, of course, the system is large and complicated. Second, the implementation of each event and program is heavily influenced by its context. The energy and interest of the schools and teachers amplify or diminish the effects of training events. Third, staff development influences its ultimate goal, student learning, through a chain of events. Content of high potential needs good training design if it is to come to life in the classroom to a degree that can achieve its potential. Measuring response to a series of training events by, for example, determining how participants liked them or whether initial skill and knowledge were developed provides only the beginning. If the skills are not employed and skillfully enough that student learning is affected, the chain is broken. The *entire* sequence has to be scrutinized. Fourth, the measurement of many of the important variables is technically difficult. For the implementation of training to be documented requires the collection of data by trained observers. Frequently tests of student behavior and learning have to be constructed—some of the most-used commercially-available instruments are not appropriate for all the objectives that we may have. Fifth, cost limitations almost always result in designs where a sample rather than the entire population is studied. We definitely favor the thorough study of a sample rather than a more superficial study of the entire population because the chain of events and moderating variables can only be tracked by the collection and analysis of high-quality data. Sixth, good evaluation runs against the normative practices that are termed "evaluations." The most common current practice is the use of opinionaires asking participants in training events to "rate" the event and often the trainers and organizers. As we reported in chapter six the opinions of personnel about training events, especially superficial ones, are very poor predictors of implementation. For example, a series of well-received lectures on a teaching practice by themselves will have relatively little effect on teaching practice. Other components are necessary to achieve an impact on practice. An "evaluation" based on opinions about the lectures could be deceiving unless implementation is scrutinized also.

In the next pages we will present a framework that permits the development of designs that include what we believe are the most important variables if we wish to evaluate program events, components, and the general health of the entire system. The entire framework includes more variables than most specific evaluation studies will be likely to include and functions as an overall conception from which a variety of evaluations can be designed.

A FRAMEWORK FOR EVALUATING STAFF DEVELOPMENT PROGRAMS

The evaluation of staff development addresses three categories of questions:

1. The first pertains to the human resource development system *qua* such. The purpose is to find out how the system is doing. Is it in good health? Does it succeed in its purposes? How well does it provide for individuals, schools, and district initiatives? Essentially, the issue is whether an active system is operating and the lives of all personnel are touched regularly by it. In the current era, when systems are being developed, we want to know about the degrees of development and what needs to be done to improve them.
2. The second category deals with the major dimensions of the system and examines the health of those dimensions. Policy-makers need to know how well individuals, schools, and system initiatives are being served and what can be done to improve those dimensions of the system.
3. The third category is concentrated on the study of specific programs and events within each of the dimensions of the system. Many specific questions can be asked in this category and only a few can be addressed by an evaluation system. The following are examples. Are programs that give teachers the opportunity to study teaching skills and strategies succeeding? Are school improvement programs being implemented,

affecting the social organization of the school as intended, and affecting the lives of the students? Are particular district initiatives being implemented and are they improving the performance of the students?

We begin with a discussion of the categories of variables that can be investigated, proceed to methods for documenting and measuring them, and finally to the design of evaluation efforts that examine the overall health of the system.

Categories of Variables

The major variables to be explored fall under the categories Teacher, School and System, Program, and Student (see Figure 4).

Figure 4. Teachers, Schools, Programs, Students: The Major Variables in Staff Development Systems

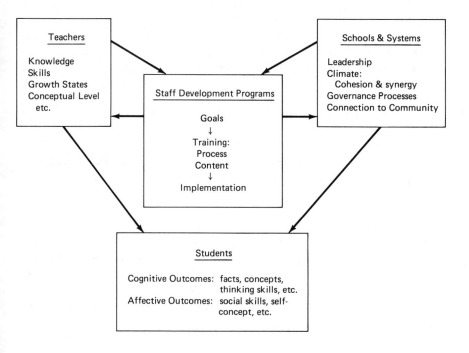

- *Individual teachers* bring to the staff development situation their current knowledge and skills, their teaching styles, and personal characteristics such as states of growth, conceptual level, and concepts of selves. They also bring perceptions about their needs and preferences for certain kinds of staff development. The study of teachers can be designed to provide information that can have several uses. One is to determine *needs* as, for example, what teaching strategies are and are not in existing repertoires, and what knowledge about academic subjects is needed. Another is to provide *baselines* against which we can measure progress. For example, if the purpose of a program is to help personnel expand their repertoire of skills and strategies, their current repertoire provides the starting point against which success can be measured. Third is to generate information about variables that can *moderate* effects. For example, persons in various states of growth are likely to respond differently to particular offerings.
- *Schools and school systems* can be characterized by types of leadership, the cohesion and synergy of their social systems, the governance processes they employ, and their relationships with the communities they serve. These variables can also function as needs assessments, as baselines, and as moderators. For example, the study of cohesion can serve to identify needs, can become a baseline when cohesion is the objective of a program, and can be examined as a moderator when the program interacts with the social system of the school, as when a peer coaching program is implemented.
- *Staff development programs* can be defined by the goals and objectives they seek to accomplish, including the content and the processes employed in training, and the degrees of implementation intended. The goals are the source of the dependent variables of an evaluation — whether teaching skills and strategies, knowledge about academic content, student learning, or the other designed outcomes of the program or program elements.
- *Students* also bring to the educational setting existing knowledge, skills, and personal characteristics which can be studied to determine goals and program structure, operate as baselines, and which also moderate treatments.

All these variables tend to interact in reciprocal fashions; that is, they affect each other, and in ways we do not often acknowledge when designing and evaluating staff development programs. Consider, for example, the categories *Teachers* and *Staff Development Programs* in Figure 4. The knowledge and skills teachers possess often determine the content of training programs, at least in systems where teachers are consulted regarding their needs for training. The perceptual world of the teachers can become the perceptual world of the program. Teachers' states of growth, conceptual levels and self-concepts partially determine the social climate of training events. Less than charismatic trainers working with good substance and a preponderance of interested and energetic teachers can have a highly successful training experience with good levels of attention, participation, and interaction. On the other hand, the most skillful trainers can have difficulty communicating with individuals who actively push away new ideas. In either case, however, if knowledge and skill are not sufficiently developed during training to sustain practice in the classroom, implementation of new skills is unlikely.

In the course of the implementation of a staff development program or even a specific program element, the variables pertaining to teachers, schools and systems, and programs can be altered, which sometimes confounds evaluation, although the problem should not dismay us.

For example, a program is *designed* to affect teachers and a successful one does so. Under optimal conditions, training processes result in increased knowledge and skills that can affect the response to the events. (Success breeds success.) In other words, the training content and process that can, over the long term, positively affect students, also affects the teachers. States of growth (see chapter ten) can be enhanced by the synergy and commitment to practice generated by a preponderantly outreaching and active group of teachers. Conceptual level, although unlikely to change as a result of a single training experience, can move upward for those involved in intensive, long-term staff development programs that not only introduce new and complex substance but work as well on transfer of training to classroom instruction. Essentially, effective staff development programs bring about change and growth in teachers, just as effective instructional programs bring about change and growth in students.

Schools both bring their characteristics to the staff development situation and can be affected by those programs. Schools are dynamic social systems. Their dimensions are hard to measure but yield to persistent effort. Both teachers and students can tell you if their school is a good place to work, an upbeat or friendly place, if people care for each other, if they are treated fairly, if their school has a good reputation, and so on (see chapters three and four). Researchers studying schools thought to be more effective have concluded that schools that hold high expectations for students, are affirmative toward them, have clear missions and well-defined curriculums, and have strong norms regarding achievement are more likely to influence the social and academic development of their students. Variables like these hold multiple implications for the design and evaluation of staff development programs, whether those programs are aimed at individuals, schools or systems, or combinations of these clienteles. Powerful instructional leaders who actively encourage growth in curriculum and instruction are likely to seek out promising ideas in both teaching process and instructional content, and thus seek staff development opportunities for their faculties. They pull energy and resources toward their schools. It is not uncommon to find disproportionate amounts of district staff development budgets concentrated in some schools simply because other schools believe they have no need for the resources or because they have fewer ideas about how to use them.

Reciprocally, staff development programs are much more likely to operate effectively in schools with active instructional leaders and positive social climates and also to have an affirmative effect in those environments. Teachers and principals who have learned how to act collectively in the planning and execution of school improvement programs are in a position to use staff development offerings productively and organize the follow-up activities that facilitate transfer of training. For example, Showers' (1980) study of teacher efficacy found large differences in opportunity for school improvement activity, staff development, and participation in decision making among the high schools in a single school district where, officially, the available resources were equal. The governance processes and the organization of study groups and peer coaching communities that we have been advocating in this book are not only vehicles for implementing staff development systems smoothly and increasing the probability of the transfer of new skills and knowledge. They are also designed to improve the organizational climates of the schools and the states of growth of the personnel as well. In other words, strong staff development programs both interact with the characteristics of the schools and affect them. Again, success breeds success. Strong programs become even more powerful because they affect the social contexts in which they must operate.

Finally, staff development programs have opportunities to affect students through their impacts on teachers and schools. A whole range of curriculums, teaching strategies, and social climate variables are capable of achieving the cognitive and affective aims we hold for students. We discussed in chapter four some of the options available for staff development content, and in chapter six the training designs most likely to result in implementation. We believe it is possible, with present knowledge and technology, to study growth in education's "bottom line" – student learning – and we believe that no serious evaluation should fail to include student learning as a dependent variable. Generally, long-term implementations of curriculums and models of teaching have greater effects than shorter ones, partly because the initial gains enable the students to respond more effectively to the curricular and instructional strategies. Also, well-implemented curriculums and technologies bring energy to the learning environment that may have effects broader than the designed ones. Perhaps this is why the implementation of aesthetics curriculums has in some cases been accompanied by increases in student achievement in areas like reading.

DOCUMENTATION AND MEASUREMENT

Before we consider the design of evaluation projects we need to consider the nature of data collection with respect to the variables.

Getting Started: Documentation

Documentation (description of people, schools, systems, and students) of the variables pertaining to individuals, schools, school systems, and students is essential to any evaluation design. Documentation of the nature of the programs as actually carried out follows close behind.

If existing conditions can affect the design and implementation of staff development programs as well as being affected by them, evaluation designs need to begin with the documentation of the current state of individuals, schools and systems, and students. Ultimately this is necessary to determine what, if any, changes can be attributed to staff development initiatives. Documentation of existing conditions also enables predictions about current programs and assists in the development of new ones (a process commonly referred to in evaluation circles as "formative" evaluation).

For individuals, one might assess existing knowledge and skill with regard to academic content and teaching process, and states of growth (see chapter ten). Variables of interest in relation to the school might include descriptions of leadership patterns, governance structures, relations with the community, and the social climate, including the nature of interactions between teachers, teachers and administrators, and all staff with students. A thorough documentation of the existing health of schools and the teachers within them provides a solid base for planning, including needs and goals, types of training, and desired outcomes for students.

Documentation of present staff development systems should include a thorough analysis of present programs — training processes employed, content offered, clientele served, and whether offerings are interfaced with individual school improvement plans. Armed with descriptions of individuals, schools and systems, and staff development programs, the reciprocal influence of each upon the other should begin to emerge, thus providing grist for the design-development-implementation-evaluation mill. Predictions about the effects of current programs, given research on training processes and various types of content, can guide evaluation efforts.

Measurement

Whether a program seeks to document and describe conditions or measure various factors in a search for correlational or cause and effect relationships, attention must be paid to measurement techniques. An impressive array of instruments exists for measuring a plethora of variables – Table 3 lists examples of existing instruments. The development and validation of evaluation instruments is a highly technical field and we strongly recommend consultation with experts when designing serious evaluation efforts. There are existing instruments, however, that can be used by most education personnel. The safest caveat is to triangulate data collection, e.g., collect data from multiple sources and perspectives in relation to specific questions.

- *Interviews.* Interview data are useful for documenting teachers' existing familiarity with various teaching processes, calculating States of Growth (see Table 3), determining feelings and beliefs about the school's social climate, and for gathering descriptions and perceptions of governance structures and leadership styles. Interview data can also be used, in conjunction with other measures, to determine levels of implementation of an innovation.
- *Observation.* Observational data are needed to measure skill levels and transfer of training variables, not because self-reports are dishonest but because it is difficult to estimate one's level of skill without some metric for comparison. Most teachers rarely see other teachers work and therefore have little notion of what they themselves do well or poorly in relation to others or some criterion. In our studies, we found that even extremely skillful teachers routinely underestimated their competence and ability and focused on their (perceived) shortcomings. Observations of students working in instructional settings that make new and different demands on them are useful for determining student needs for skill development in order to function successfully with the cognitive and social demands of the environment.
- The use of observation instruments generally requires the training of observers to a criterion of reliability. Instruments differ widely in their complexity and consequently in the training required to use them

Table 3. Instruments for Measuring Staff Development Variables

Name	Purpose	Type	Reference
CASES (Classroom analysis schedule for educational settings)	Student coping styles	Category system, observation	Spaulding, R.L.(1974)
STARS (Spaulding Teachers Activity Rating Schedule)	Teaher behavior	Category system, observation	Spaulding, R.L. (1978)
FLACCS (Florida Climate & Control System)	Classroom interaction	Sign system, observation	Soar, R.S., Soar, R.M., & Ragosta, M.(1971)
OScAR SV	Classroom interaction	Category system, observation	Medley, D.M. & Mitzel, H. (1955)
TIS (Teacher Innovator System)	Classroom interaction	Category system, observation	Joyce, B.R. (1980)
Myers-Briggs Type Indicator	Personality variables	Paper & pencil test, self-report	Myers, I.B. (1980)
Conceptual Level	Personality variables	Paper & pencil test, self-report	Hunt, D. et al. (1978)
CBAM (Concerns Based Adoption Model)	Concers about and use of innovations	Interview, questionnaire	Loucks, NewLove, & Hall (1975)
Growth States	Levels of participation in staff development activities	Interview, questionnaire	Joyce, Bush, McKibbin (1982)
School Improvement Questionnaire	Health & activity of school, readiness for staff development	Questionnaire	Joyce, Bush, McKibbin (1982)
Leader Behavior Description Questionnaire	Principal leadership styles	Self-report response to paper & pencil test	Halpin, A.W. (1966)

reliably. Well-developed instruments exist for examining a broad range of teacher and student variables in the classroom. We recommend the use of instruments that have established reliability and validity data whenever possible. The design of new observation instruments is complex, time-consuming and expensive (see Table 3). Although common sense tells us that teachers intuitively "know" what to look for, observation instruments developed from teachers' perceptions about what should be studied have had a relatively small payoff (Medley, et al., 1981) and in some cases aspects of instruction that teachers thought would correlate with student learning have actually had negative correlations. This does not mean that teachers do not have wisdom about teaching so much as that they need training in the technology of the study of teaching to translate their wisdom into usable instruments.

- *Questionnaires/Inventories.* Questionnaires and inventories are useful for documenting past training histories and perceptions of leadership styles. In addition, many personality dimensions (e.g., Conceptual Level, Myers-Briggs) are computed from questionnaires and inventories (see Table 3). While the scoring of inventories must often be contracted to experts, administration of the instruments is frequently possible on site without special training. Furthermore, many schools and districts have psychologists on their staffs trained in the administration of personality questionnaires and inventories.

- *Document Analysis.* Documents are a rich source of evaluation data. Documents include everything from minutes of Board of Education meetings, administrative councils, faculty meetings, and curriculum committees to lesson plans and instructional materials. Analysis of these documents can enlarge the picture gained from interviews, questionnaires, and observation with respect to teaching process, degrees of implementation of new practices and materials, and school and district governance processes

- *Tests of Student Learning.* Designs that include student learning require extreme care. Optimally, tests are constructed to measure precisely the outcomes that are sought. For example, if teachers study methods for teaching concepts to students, a good design is to ask them to teach a unit, say in the social studies, with and without their new strategy and build tests to determine whether the method has the desired effect—more concepts learned and a higher rate of retention of concepts and information. However, test construction is technically difficult and can be very expensive. Oddly enough, given that student learning is their business, relatively few districts have on staff experienced and highly trained measurement experts. Most districts rely on commercially-available standardized tests. When they do so, they need to make sure that the tests are appropriate to the outcomes being sought. In the case immediately above, the tests must include concepts. If the tests include few concepts, the model-relevant outcomes of conceptual models cannot be assessed by their use. Even in the domain of information, mass-testing includes very few items on any given topic within a curriculum area and one must ensure that there are enough relevant items to build a relevant sub-test. Second, test administration must be standardized and personnel other than the instructors should administer them. Third, pre- and post-tests must be given to all students involved. Fourth, only raw scores should be used. Conversion to standard scores, percentile ranks or grade-level equivalents introduces sources of error that can be misleading. (We examined the data from a district that had reported an increase from an average 30th percentile score on a particular test to the 80th, in terms of the district's rank in its state, only to find that the change was due to an increase of just seven raw score points on a test of 200 items! An increase of three and a half percent correct items was magnified by the conversion to percentile ranks.) Finally, when interpreting results it needs to be made clear that small fluctuations are common. Nearly any additional attention given to a school will normally result in a gain of about 0.2 of a standard deviation, which for a population of 50 or more will probably be statistically significant. An innovation introduced through staff development needs to exceed that magnitude before we can infer that it was due to the content and process of the innovation.

The Most Common Error: Overreliance on Opinions

The reader may have noticed that up to this point we have not mentioned the most commonly used evaluation instrument employed by staff developers to determine the success of their programs.

We will try to explain our omission.

At present, the effectiveness of most staff development offerings is estimated by means of opinion polls distributed either during or at the close of a training session. Participants are asked a variety of questions to which they respond on a five-point scale. The questions range from the attractiveness and/or effectiveness of the speaker and the training materials to the conditions of the training setting and refreshments they also often include estimates of the degree to which personal objectives were met by the training and predictions about practicality and potential usefulness.

Presumably the purpose of evaluation is the collection of data upon which to base decisions. The evaluation of a staff development experience brings us full circle to the purpose for which the experience was designed. Was the purpose to build awareness of an area and/or develop skills that could be used in the classroom? Was the purpose to provide an enjoyable experience for participants, to refine existing skills, to stretch trainees with new and challenging material? Current evaluation practice leads us to believe that questions of who presenters should be and what substance ought to be provided, where and when training should be conducted and for what duration can most readily be determined from the data collected. It is difficult to understand, however, how present evaluation practices relate to purposes.

If indeed the results of "opinionaire" evaluations of staff development activities are used to determine the effectiveness of past offerings and the planning of future offerings, several artifacts are built into the evaluation cycle.

One is that it tends to perpetuate the use of familiar offerings. For whatever reasons (and we have suggested several), teachers often report that the content in staff development programs was already familiar to them (Gall, et al., 1982). On the other hand, they tend overwhelmingly to rate highly their satisfaction with staff development activities and their effects on their students (Gall, et al., 1982). We interpret the apparent paradox of attributing positive student effects to inservice programs in which already known material is covered as the very human tendency to seek reassurance that what one is doing is the right and proper thing. There is comfort in the familiar. Reviewing what is known takes less time than introducing new material and fits more easily into existing time allocations for staff development activities. For developers and providers, there is safety in sidestepping the discomfort that accompanies new learning. Consequently, it is common to see a popular speaker passed by word of mouth from district to district and state to state, along with the presenter's evaluations from prior engagements. The implications for the introduction of content such as that described in chapter four are clear.

Another potential outcome of the opinionaire evaluation procedure is the eventual feeling that "we know everything worth knowing in this field". The circular process set up by high evaluations of safe material, which results in more of the same, gradually leads teachers to the impression that, because everything presented to them in staff development sessions is familiar, they must know everything that is worth knowing. In a field where research is adding to our knowledge of what is possible at an astounding rate, complacency with existing knowledge, even extensive existing knowledge, is hardly the norm we want to develop.

If, at the end of a training session, satisfaction with training and predictions about use are collected from participants, information about eventual use of knowledge or skill gained from training is lost to evaluators. If purposes of staff development are not tied to evaluation, there is little basis for determining if purposes have been met.

DESIGN OF EVALUATIONS

Let us now consider some examples of evaluation designs for examining the impact of staff development programs on individuals, schools and entire systems.

Benefits to Individuals of a Staff Development Program

Thirty teachers (representing twelve schools) in a district which employed 1200 teachers volunteered to participate in a teaching strategies training program. The program was offered by a local university, and participation was motivated by interest in building personal teaching repertoire, the urging of school principals, and the incentive of university credit. The objectives of the training program were limited to the acquisition and implementation of several new teaching strategies for the individuals participating. School effects were not expected, since at most two or three teachers from a single school were involved in the training.

The effectiveness of the training program was determined initially by skill levels (the ability of individuals to demonstrate the new teaching strategies) and eventually by transfer of training (appropriate and consistent use of the new strategies to meet educational objectives).

Baseline data were collected by interviewing teachers regarding their typical instructional practices and by observing classroom teaching several times over a two-week period. The purpose for collecting baseline data was simply to document that the content of training was indeed new to the teachers involved. Skill levels were determined by analysis of the discrepancy between actual and ideal performance of the new instructional strategies, as measured by an observation instrument. Transfer of training measures were a combination of performance on a two-week unit, analysis of use over a three-month period (as determined by lesson plans and interviews), and students' familiarity and comfort with the cognitive and social demands of the new strategies.

The example above is a much more complex evaluation of training than is normally completed for district-sponsored staff development programs for which individual teachers volunteer. It is not unusual, however, for a university-sponsored program in which research questions are being addressed.

A School-based Staff Development Program

A high school in a large urban district designed a school improvement plan with increased teaching repertoire as its central theme. An extremely energetic principal arranged for his staff to be introduced to a number of current concepts in instruction, including student learning styles, higher order thinking processes, cooperative learning and alternative models of teaching. The district had no staff development thrust and almost no staff development budget. To pay for these "awareness" sessions for his staff, the principal approached a foundation with a proposal for staff development and school improvement and received a small grant for his project. He then invited several neighboring districts to send two to three representatives to sessions and charged them "tuition" for their participation. He recruited so successfully that the revenue more than paid for the initial events.

A collaborative governance structure was developed from an existing curriculum committee which represented all high school departments. With the principal and his administrative staff, this committee chose a staff development focus for the next two years – the increase of teaching repertoire that would encourage higher order thinking skills and cooperative study while providing a variety of learning environments sensitive to student learning style preferences.

Since staff development efforts of this magnitude were unheard of in this district, the committee was concerned that students and parents would view the time spent in training as time subtracted from the "regular" instructional program. A three-pronged program of activities and public relations was designed to communicate purposes of the program to the community. First, students were involved in community-improvement projects and their efforts were highly publicized. Second, area media were bombarded with reports of student achievement in all areas – sports, music, academic and industrial subjects. Third, a moribund teacher-parent organization was revived, which served as a two-way conduit between the school and the community with respect to goals for the school. At the end of the first year, polls of the community showed that this particular high school was seen as a caring place where students had a chance to develop their potential and get a decent education and that furthermore, this high school was populated by more mature young citizens than other high schools in the area.

Measures of individual teacher characteristics as well as school climate resulted in a mixed picture at the beginning of the project. The entire school staff (teachers, administrators, counselors, nurses, secretaries, cafeteria workers, bus drivers, custodians, etc.) responded to a personality inventory that yielded a profile regarding (adult) learning style and social interaction preferences. Feedback to the staff on the results of this instrument provided a common language for discussing and acknowledging individual differences during the planning and implementation of training activities. Climate measures revealed high rates of satisfaction with school administration, feelings by both teachers and students that their school was a good one in which to work, and a focus on strengths rather than weaknesses. Cohesion among students was higher than among teachers, although neither was at the top of the scale. As in many schools, a small group of energetic teachers with high levels of activity left the impression with casual observers that the entire faculty was highly energetic. Interviews to assess states of growth, however, revealed a normal distribution, that is, some teachers who were actively seeking professional growth opportunities, some who were actively avoiding such opportunities, and a majority of teachers who were somewhat passive in their response to growth options provided by their environments. Observation revealed that the teaching repertoire of this experienced faculty was almost entirely confined to the recitation, with some sprinkling of inquiry processes in the science department.

As the staff development committee began to plan the process by which they would meet their goal of increased teaching repertoire, several crucial decisions were made. First, with an eye on their budget, they decided to develop a cadre of trainers from within their own ranks. Their notion was to develop a group of highly skilled teacher/trainers that could then provide training to the rest of the faculty. Second, they consulted with their consultant/trainers before training began to negotiate time and cost required to develop a skillful cadre and allocated resources first to training. Third, they designed a follow-up, peer-coaching program to assist implementation of newly learned skills and strategies, reasoning that eventual faculty-wide training would be enhanced by the presence of a functioning, observable teaching-strategies laboratory within the school.

Existing data on student achievement were quite traditional, consisting of standardized test scores for 9th and 11th graders and writing samples hand scored on a list of criteria similar to those employed by the Bay Area Writers Project. Although the initial goal of the staff development project was increased teaching repertoire for teachers, eventually student outcomes would be of interest. One of the most difficult tasks was to decide which students to study and what kinds of learning would be the focus.

Because only 15 teachers from the one high school were part of the training cadre (other members were from nearby districts who were paying for the service they received), the committee knew they could not look for a school-wide effect on student learning during the first two years of the program when only the cadre had reached full implementation. A limited evaluation of student effects was conducted, however. First, the committee decided to focus evaluation on only the cognitive and affective outcomes predicted by research to result from the teaching strategies covered by the training. This meant adding criterion-referenced tests to the existing norm-referenced tests already in use and expanding the administration of the standardized tests to grades 10 and 12. Second, they allowed the cadre one year to work on their own skills before approaching the question of student achievement. This provided an opportunity to check implementation of new strategies in the classrooms of the cadre at the beginning of the second year before choosing a testing sample. Third, a sample of students was selected who had only cadre teachers for their instruction in English, math, social studies and science. (All departments were represented in the cadre.) Thus both standard and criterion-referenced test results could be used in the analysis of student outcomes.

The evaluation design described above certainly can be criticized from several points of view. It is, however, in our opinion a reasonable, thoughtful and ambitious effort, given very limited resources and the uniqueness of this school's effort within the context of its district staff development and evaluation programs.

EVALUATING A SYSTEMIC INITIATIVE

About five years ago a large state developed a network of regional centers focusing on special education and organized to deliver training to assist in the mainstreaming process. These centers designed staff development offerings and made them known throughout their regions. Some of the offerings were for special education teachers and others were for other faculty and administrators.

A documentation of participation and the nature of the offerings proved to be highly useful. From the documentation it was discovered that nearly all of the participants were special education teachers, even when the offerings were designed for "regular" classroom teachers. Thus the centers were missing one of their primary clienteles. Second, the training process for 90 percent of the offerings was information only, and primarily information about the state and federal laws relevant to the mainstreaming of special education students. The remainder of the content dealt with knowledge about children and teaching strategies that might benefit them. Finally, case studies of several schools in the areas being served indicated that faculty and administration were extremely anxious about mainstreaming and some were quite suspicious of it. Also, the new resource teachers in those schools were regarded with suspicion and their help was rejected by many of the teachers.

In that case the collection of evaluation data did not need to proceed further to provide a basis for reorientation of the programs offered by those centers. It was easy to judge that the programs were probably having little impact and that new training content and designs, and fresh ways of helping the schools deal with their problems would have to be found, not to mention ways of reaching more teachers and administrators. Detailed assessment of teacher behavior and student learning as a result of those offerings would have been costly and futile.

SUMMARY

Evaluation is important and difficult. In current practice documentation is underused and opinionnaires are overused. Measurement of student achievement requires a technical expertise not available in many settings. With all the difficulties, however, it is an exciting area and many fine instruments are available as well as good designs for those with the patience to use them. If we truly intend to increase student learning through staff development programs, serious evaluation of those programs will be necessary.

CHAPTER TEN

THE STATES OF GROWTH OF PEOPLE IN THE ORGANIZATION

Although people and their growth are the important substance of this book, this is the first chapter that attempts to deal conceptually with the most important element in the equations of staff development. And people are much on the minds of the persons who organize and carry out staff development programs. Witness the amount of time spent in worrying about uncooperative people and the provisions for incentives and rewards for participating personnel.

We have made a number of statements about people, however, and as we directly approach the subject it is worthwhile to summarize some of them.

- First of all, the training research is affirmative in that it suggests that teachers are capable learners and are able to master a wide range of curricular and instructional strategies and use them effectively in the classroom. This is a strong statement about education personnel, so often maligned as burned out, aging, academically impoverished (Vance and Schlecty, 1985), and as working under intolerable conditions (McLaughlin, 1986). Although we are in favor of recruiting the best possible talent into education and providing them with the conditions under which they will flourish, we are very pleased with the capability of present personnel, especially because the time of initial preparation is so meager and its quality is so suspect. Teachers have lots of learning ability.

- Second, it appears that staff development programs can be designed to allow teachers to increase their learning capability. Essentially, the more skills teachers develop and the more they widen their repertoire, the greater their ability to master an even greater range of skills and strategies.
- Third, teachers have the very human tendency to respond affirmatively to a positive social and organizational climate. Faculties that are organized into study and coaching teams and which work together for the improvement of the school are more cohesive, have higher morale, and are more responsive to initiatives from one another and from administrative leadership.

It is essential that the definition of the responsibilities of teaching include the role as faculty member much more prominently than it has in the past. Teachers who have worked in relative isolation naturally concentrate on their roles as organizer of the classroom and as instructor. However, both school improvement and systemic initiatives require collective action. And the study of teaching, even for individuals working on their skills and knowledge, is greatly facilitated by contact with others.

INDIVIDUAL DIFFERENCES

However, we need a frame of reference that will enable us to think about individual differences in personnel and to take those differences into account.

There are a number of ways of thinking about individual differences that are candidates for our use at the present time. Some of these have been developed to help us think about the learning styles of children (Dunn & Dunn, 1975; Gregorc, 1982; McCarthy, 1981) and can be applied to adults as well. Some developed to distinguish various styles of thinking (e.g., Myers, 1962) and examine how those styles affect problem solving. There is at least one current theory that attempts to describe differences between children and adults as learners (Knowles, 1978).

A number of broad conceptualizations of personality can be applied to the behavior of teachers as instructors and as learners (Harvey, Hunt, & Schroeder, 1961; Maslow, 1962; Erikson, 1950). Especially Conceptual Systems Theory (Hunt, 1971) has been heavily studied and has been a useful predictor of teacher-student interaction, the breadth of styles employed by teachers, sensitivity to students and responsiveness to them, and, most pertinent here, aptitude to acquire the competence to use teaching skills and strategies (Joyce, Brown, & Peck, Eds., 1981).

In this chapter we will discuss a framework that was developed from the study of the professional and personal lives of teachers in the California Staff

Development Study (Joyce, Bush, & McKibbin, 1981, 1982, 1984). The framework was developed to guide practice in the organization of human resource development programs and school improvement efforts (McKibbin & Joyce, 1980; Joyce, Hersh, & McKibbin, 1983). Although it was developed from a strictly practical orientation, the findings are correlated with the theories of personality growth and take conceptual development, self concept, and psychological maturity into account.

THE CONCEPT OF STATE OF GROWTH

As we indicated earlier, the framework was developed during a large-scale longitudinal study of staff development and school improvement practices in California. The objective was to obtain a detailed picture of the opportunities for growth experienced by teachers from their school setting, the district, universities, intermediate agencies (county offices of education and professional development centers), and other institutions. Case studies were made of more than 300 teachers from 21 districts in seven counties and more than 2,000 others were surveyed through questionnaires. In addition to information about participation in the formal systems of support (courses, workshops, and the services of administrators and supervisors), interaction with peers was examined as were those aspects of personal lives that might have implications for professional growth. Thus, data were collected on what came to be termed the formal, the peer-generated, and the personal domains, depending on the origins of the activities that people engaged in.

The focus was the dynamic of individual interaction with the environment. The thesis was that within any given environment (say, a school in the San Francisco Bay area), opportunities for productive interaction leading to growth would theoretically be about equal. That is, formal staff development systems, colleagues, and opportunities to read, attend films and events in the performing arts, engage in athletic activity, etc. would be available to all personnel in profusion. Thus, differences in activity would be a function of the individual's disposition to interact productively with the environment. If we discovered differences, we could proceed to try to understand their origins and develop ideas for capitalizing on them.

THE FORMAL, PEER-GENERATED, AND PERSONAL DOMAINS

The amount of interaction in all three domains varied greatly. The differences were vast in both urban and rural areas and among elementary and secondary teachers. They are easily illustrated in regions like the Bay Area and the Los Angeles Basin where literally thousands of courses and workshops are available. Most principals and supervisors have been trained to provide active clinical support, many professional development centers in county offices and other agencies involve teachers in the selection of staff development opportunities and there are active organizations of teachers of writing, science, and other curriculum areas. In addition, of course, the opportunities for personal activity of all sorts abound in these great metropolitan areas, which also are close to mountain ranges, waterways, and oceans. The nature of the differences in each domain is interesting.

Formal Staff Development Opportunities

Participation ranged from persons who experienced only the activities sponsored and required by the district (possibly only one or two workshops or presentations and one or two visits by supervisors or consultants) and who were aware of very few options to very active, aware persons with definite plans of professional enhancement. A small number effectively exploited the opportunities in universities and the larger teacher centers.

Peer-Generated Opportunities for Growth

The range here was from persons who had virtually no professional discussions with any other teachers to persons who had close and frequent interaction, experienced mentoring relationships (on the giving or receiving end or both) and who gathered with others to instigate the introduction of innovations or initiatives for the improvement of the school.

The Personal Domain

In their personal lives some teachers were extremely active, with one or two well-developed areas of participation and others made virtually no use of the rich environments in which they lived. We found some very active readers and others who barely skim the headlines of the daily paper, some Sierra Club activists and others who had never visited Yosemite, some members of performing arts groups and others who have not seen a film or a live performance in 10 years or more.

STATES OF GROWTH

Somewhat to our surprise, the levels of activity were correlated across domains. That is, those who were more active professionally were also more active personally. Looking for reasons, we concluded that the differences in levels of activity were produced by the individuals' orientations toward their environments, moderated by social influence.

Orientations toward the Environment

The essence of the concept is the degree to which the environment is viewed as an opportunity for satisfying growth. Thus the more active people view the environment as a set of possibilities for satisfying interaction. They initiate contact and exploit the possibilities. Less active persons are less aware of the possibilities or more indifferent to them. The least active persons expend energy protecting themselves from what they see as a threatening or unpleasant environment, avoiding contact and fending off the initiatives of others. Also, the persons who are more active and more initiating are also more proactive. That is, they draw more attention from the environment, bringing more possibilities within their reach. This phenomenon multiplies the opportunities for many people. It was not unusual for us to discover that certain schools that were characterized by a cluster of active people (and generally by an active principal) were regularly approached by central office personnel, teacher centers, and universities to be the trial sites for everything from computer technology to community involvement programs. Those people and their schools receive more resources and training while some schools, characterized by a cluster of resistant persons, were approached last, and many initiatives passed them by.

Social Influence

Close friends and colleagues, and the social climate of the workplace and the neighborhood, moderate the general dispositions toward growth. Affirmative and active friends and colleagues and positive social climates induce persons to engage in greater activity than they would if left to themselves. This finding provides another dimension to the general theme of chapter three. The synergistic environment is not only essential for collective action but to generate the kind of colleagueship that will be productive for the states of growth of individuals.

Also, as we will emphasize later, a major goal of a human resource development system is to increase the states of growth of the personnel in the system, potentially benefiting the individuals as well as the organization and ensuring that the children are in contact with more active, seeking personalities.

LEVELS OF ACTIVITY

Although the orientations toward growth are best represented on a continuum, people gradually, over time, develop patterns that have more clearly discernible edges and it is not unreasonable to categorize them, provided we recognize that the categories blend into one another. With that caveat, the following prototypes are presented because they can be useful in explaining behavior and in planning staff development programs and organizing faculties to exploit them vigorously.

A Gourmet Omnivore

Our prototypes here are mature high-activity people who have learned to canvass the environment and exploit it successfully.

In the formal domain they keep aware of the possibilities for growth, identify high-probability events, and work hard at squeezing them for their growth potential.

They constitute the hard-core clientele for teacher centers and arrays of district and intermediate-agency offerings for volunteers. They initiate ideas for offerings and find ways of influencing the policy-makers. However, they are not negative toward system initiatives. They have the complexity to balance their personal interests with the awareness that they belong to an organization.

Our prototype omnivores find kindred souls with whom to interact professionally. They learn from informal interaction with their peers. A group of omnivores may work together and generate initiatives or attend workshops or courses together. When the computer appeared on the educational scene it was often groups of omnivores who learned to use them and developed the computer centers in their schools.

It is in their personal lives that our prototype omnivores become most clearly defined. They are characterized by a general high level of awareness, but the distinguishing feature is one or two areas in which they are enthusiastically involved. These areas vary quite a bit from person to person. One may be an omnivorous reader; another a theatergoer; a third an avid backpacker or skier; a fourth a maker of ceramics; some run businesses. In close consort with others they generate activities. The spouses of omnivore tennis players are likely to find themselves with rackets in their hands and the close friends of moviegoers will be importuned to share films. Because of their reactivity, our mature omnivores have learned to fend off opportunities and protect time for their chosen avocations.

What is striking is their habit of both exploiting and enriching whatever environment they find themselves in. In the workplace, they strive to learn all they can about their craft and give and take energy from their peers. In their private lives they find opportunities for development.

They are also distinguished by their persistence. In McKibbin & Joyce's (1980) study they both sought training that would have a high likelihood for transfer and, once back in the workplace, practiced and created the conditions of peer support that enabled them to implement a remarkably high proportion of the skills to which they were exposed. They are also more likely than others to bring the ideas they gain in their personal lives into the workplace and use them in their teaching.

A Passive Consumer

About 10 percent of the persons we studied fit the profile of our Gourmet Omnivores, and another 10 percent were somewhat less active, although still quite engaged with aspects of their environment. By far the largest number, however, (about 70 percent) resembled the prototype we term the Passive Consumer.

The distinguishing characteristics of our passive consumers are a more or less amiable conformity to the environment and a high degree of dependence on the immediate social context. In other words their degree of activity depends greatly on who they are with. In the company of other passive consumers, our prototype is relatively inactive. We studied one school in which all of the personnel in one wing of the building were passive, and their interchange with others was amiable but involved few serious discussions about teaching and learning. They visited one another's classrooms rarely. None attended staff development activities that were not required by the administration. They had no objections to being required to attend those workshops, one day in the Fall and one in the Spring, and they enjoyed them, but did nothing with the content.

In another wing of the school two passive consumers found themselves in the company of two omnivores and an active consumer and were drawn into many of the activities generated by their more enterprising colleagues. They found themselves helping to set up computer workstations for the students, cooperating in scheduling and the selection of software, learning word processing and how to teach their students to use self-instructional programs. They attended workshops on the teaching of writing with the study group instigated by the omnivores and began revamping their writing programs.

In personal life our prototype passive consumer is also dependent on consort. If they have relatively inactive spouses and extended families, they will be relatively inactive. If they are with relatives, friends, and neighbors who initiate activity, their levels of activity will increase.

A Reticent Consumer

Whereas our passive consumer has a relatively amiable, if rather unenterprising, view of the world, about 10 percent of the persons we studied expend energy actually pushing away opportunities for growth. We speak of these persons as Reticent because they have developed an orientation of reluctance to interact positively with their cultural environment. We can observe this dynamic in both professional and domestic settings.

Our prototype reticent attends only the staff development that is required and is often angry about having to be there, deprecates the content, whatever it is, and tries to avoid follow-up activities. Our reticent treats administrative initiatives and those from peers with equal suspicion and tends to believe that negative attitudes are justified because "the system" is inherently oppressive and unfeeling. Thus even peers who make initiatives are deprecated because they are "naive" if they believe that they will gain administrative support for their idealistic notions. Hence our reticent tends to view our omnivores as negatively as they do the hated administration. The hard-core reticent even rejects opportunities for involvement in decision making, regarding them as coopting moves by basically malign forces.

In discussion about personal lives the structure of attitudes was similar. Our reticents tend to emphasize what they see as defects in people, institutions, services, and opportunities in a range of fields. Film, theater, athletic activity, state and national parks, books and newspapers all are suffering rapid decay. ("Only trash gets published these days. Movies are full of sex and violence.") In the richness of an urban environment they tend to emphasize crowding as an obstacle to participation to events. ("If I could get tickets. If you didn't have to wait for a court. You can never get in to the good movies.") In the rural environments it is lack of facilities that is to blame.

Even so, our reticent is not unaffected by the immediate social context. In affirmative school climates they do not act out their negative views as much. In the company of omnivores they can be carried along in school improvement efforts. Affirmative spouses who tolerate their jaundiced opinions good-naturedly involve them in a surprising number of activities. In the right circumstances they learn to take advantage of the opportunities in their lives.

CONCEPTUAL STRUCTURE, SELF CONCEPT, AND STATES OF GROWTH

In an attempt to seek reasons for the differences in states of growth manifested by the teachers we were studying we turned to a number of developmental theories. Two of them are of particular interest to us here because their descriptions of development appear to correlate with the states of growth we found (Joyce, McKibbin, & Bush, 1984). One is conceptual systems theory (Harvey, Hunt, & Schroeder, 1961; Hunt, 1971) and the other is self-concept theory (Maslow, 1962).

Conceptual Development

Conceptual systems theory describes persons in terms of the structure of concepts they use to organize information about the world. In the lowest developmental stages persons use relatively few concepts for organizing their world, tend to have dichotomous views with few "shades of grey," and much emotion is attached to their views. They tend to reject information that does not fit into their concepts or to distort it to make it fit. Thus people and events are viewed as right or wrong. Existing concepts are preserved.

At higher stages of development people develop greater ability to integrate new information, are more decentered and can tolerate alternative views better, and their conceptual structure is modified as old concepts become obsolete and new ones are developed. New experiences are tolerated and bring new information and ideas, rather than being rejected or distorted to preserve the existing state.

For example, let us consider persons at the lower and higher developmental stages on a first visit to a foreign culture. Persons characterized by the lower conceptual levels are suspicious of the different and tend to find fault with it. ("You can't *believe* what they eat there.") They peer through the windows of the tour busses with increasing gratitude that they will soon be returning to America. They speak loudly to the "stupid" hotel personnel who don't speak English. They clutch their wallets to keep them away from the conniving, dishonest natives and their unclean hands.

Their higher conceptual level companions are fascinated by the new sights, sounds, and smells. Gingerly they order the local dishes, comparing them with the familiar, finding some new and pleasing tastes, and bargaining for a recipe. They prefer to walk, avoiding the bus unless time forbids. They ask shopkeepers to pronounce the names of things. They brush off the grime to get a better look at the interesting vase in the corner. They speak quietly and wait for the hotel personnel to indicate the local custom.

There is a substantial correlation between conceptual development and the states of growth of the teachers and administrators we studied. The omnivores are in a continual search for more productive ways of organizing information and have more complex conceptual structures as a result. Their openness to new experience requires an affirmative view of the world and the conceptual sophistication to deal with the new ideas they encounter. Our passive consumers have more limited structures and less ability to figure out how to reach for new experience and deal with it. Our reticents are busy protecting their present concepts and act offended by the presence of the unfamiliar. They can be as negative toward children they do not understand as they are toward the facilitators who try to bring new ideas and techniques into their orbit. Conceptual development is correlated with variety and flexibility in teaching styles (Hunt, 1981), with ease in learning new approaches to teaching, and with ability to understand students and modulate to them (Joyce, Brown, & Peck, Eds., 1981).

A change to a more productive orientation involves a structural change — a more complex structure capable of analyzing people and events from multiple points of view and the ability to assimilate new information and accommodate to it.

Self-Concept

More than 25 years ago Abraham Maslow (1962) and Carl Rogers (1961) developed formulations of personal growth and functioning that have guided attempts since then to understand and deal with individual differences in response to the physical and social environment. Rather than concentrating on intellectual aptitude and development, their theories focused on individuals' views of self or self-concepts. They took the position that our competence to relate to the environment is greatly affected by the stances we take toward ourselves.

Strong self-concepts are accompanied by self-actualizing behavior, a reaching out toward the environment with confidence that the interaction will be productive. The self-actualizing person interacts richly with the milieu, finding opportunities for growth and enhancement and, inevitably, contributing to the development of others.

Somewhat less-developed persons feel competent to deal with the environment but accept it for what it is and are less likely to develop growth-producing relationships from their own initiatives. They work within the environment and what it brings to them rather than generating opportunities from and with it.

The least-developed persons bear a more precarious relationship with their surroundings. They are less sure of their ability to cope. Much of their energy is spent in efforts to ensure that they survive in a less-than generous world.

It is not surprising that we found a relationship between the states of growth of the people we studied and their concepts of self. Our omnivores are self-actualizing. They feel good about themselves and their surroundings. Our passive consumers feel competent but are dependent on the environment for growth-producing opportunities. Our reticents feel that they live in a precarious and threatening world. The faults that they find in their surroundings are products not of being well-developed and able to discern problems the rest of us cannot see but of an attempt to rationalize their need to protect themselves from a world of which they are afraid.

Understanding Growth and the Potential for Growth

The theories of conceptual growth and self-concept both help us understand the states of growth and ways of thinking about education personnel as growth-oriented programs are planned and carried out. They help us understand why people respond as they do and provide us with a basis for creating environments that are likely to be productive both in terms of the content of the programs and the people for whom they are intended.

STATES OF GROWTH AND PROGRAM DESIGN

As we design programs we can use information about people's states of growth to understand why people respond as they do to initiatives of various kinds, to capitalize productively on individual differences, and to try to help people in their ability to grow, not only in the technical senses that we have stressed in the previous chapters, but also in their orientations toward the world and what it offers them. During our discussion of these ways of using the study of individual differences, we will present some working hypotheses for program design, essentially principles that help us ensure that the people in the equation are treated as well as possible.

We recommend that the study of personal orientations be incorporated into the human resource development system. Whether the study utilizes the methodology for studying states of growth, or concentrates on conceptual complexity or self concept, or uses some other framework for studying individuals, we believe that information should be collected and employed to understand the human beings in the system. As a practical matter, the study will probably concentrate on a sample of people in any district, or school, or group of participants in a program. As a school principal, supervisor, staff development designer or presenter, we would want to be able to think about our clientele and try to understand why they respond to events and people as they do. Let us consider how persons in different states of growth are likely to respond to the Individual, Collective, and Systemic components of the system and how events and programs can be designed with individual differences in mind.

The Individual Component

The purpose of the Individual Component is to build an environment from which individuals and study groups can select options. We have proposed a governance system that relies greatly on surveys of individual needs and preferences, informed by information from councils and committees about options that might be productive. We can see the operation of states of growth in this governance process. Our omnivores will participate willingly and be likely to suggest options that will stretch them. Our passive consumers will participate willingly in an energized environment and will tend to suggest options within their current visions of teaching. (This, we believe, is why classroom management programs are so often mentioned in surveys of needs.) Our reticents are likely to resist the participatory governance process itself! They may even refer to it as a "trick of management" to co-opt them into voluntary participation in a process that "will be controlled by the administration anyway." Planners need to distinguish between complaints that are based on concerns about how the process is being administered and purely reticent behavior. This is not always easy. Omnivores who offer suggestions should not be confused with reticents expressing their internal state of dissatisfaction with the world.

Neither is interpreting what are suggested as program options so that they can fit the visions of persons in different states of development. Our passive consumers are most numerous so a simple counting of votes is likely to result in offerings that fit their vision but have little to offer our omnivores. With a differentiated view of the personnel it is possible to ensure that the spectrum of offerings provides possibilities for persons of different visions.

Participation in programs is also likely to be related to the states of growth of the individuals. Our omnivores are likely to participate in more programs and, once there, their active participation is likely to increase the energy and usefulness of the activities. They tend to appreciate follow-up activities. Their stronger self-concepts withstand the problems of implementation quite well and, with a little assistance from peers or supervisors, are very likely to achieve an acceptable level of transfer. On the other hand, they resent weak content and poorly-developed processes and can be quite critical of events that waste their time.

Passive consumers need encouragement to participate, but are likely to be responsive. Active study teams and the company of active peers will increase their rates and amounts of participation. They are generally cooperative and are amenable to follow-up activities, but these have to be well-organized and enthusiastically pursued by the organizers and the study groups if they are to be effective, for the passive consumers' dependence on the environment for stimulation requires support. Left alone, passive consumers will achieve a very low rate of transfer. Coaching teams composed of passive consumers will need help getting started and maintaining practice.

Reticent personnel will tend to avoid participation, even in events they have theoretically helped to plan. Whether they attend voluntary programs at all will depend heavily on the level of synergy in the school and the study groups to which they belong. How they will respond to events also will depend heavily on the synergy developed in the training sessions. In positive social climates they are less likely to manifest the automatic negativism that afflicts them. When they do respond negatively it is important to remember that their behavior is likely to be a product of poor self-images. Although they can be extremely unpleasant to deal with, they are actually not hard to manage in an affirmative social climate, because of their relative weakness. However, it is important to understand that they do have a more difficult time learning new skills and strategies (Joyce, Peck, & Brown, Eds., 1981) because their teaching strategies are more limited, their conceptual structures are more rigid and difficult to change, and their ability to understand students and respond to them is more limited. Aside from coping with their negativism, they need a great deal more help to achieve the same objective.

The Collective Component

As far as responses to governance and participation in specific program elements are concerned, the picture is similar to the one described immediately above and need not be repeated. However, the dynamics of the collective component have some distinctive features that require sensitive planning and execution and that also provide the greatest opportunity to help people develop a more productive orientation toward themselves and their growth.

It is within the school site that the organization of coaching teams, study groups, and councils take place and all three components depend heavily on these units or similar ones. It is the task of the principal to bring this organization into existence. The affirmative orientation of the omnivores will be essential. They begin with a stake in making environments productive for themselves and others. However, pity the poor principal who involves them in *pro forma* activities. When our omnivores spend energy on an enterprise, they expect it to pay off. An administrator who is less than serious will have trouble from them. However, they will respond seriously to serious initiatives and their energy will elevate the synergy in the organization.

As the structure is developed, it is wise to ensure that the omnivores are distributed relatively evenly among the study teams. They provide affirmative leadership (although they may not have formal positions) and also help neutralize the behavior of the reticent personnel. Our reticents are suspicious of our omnivores and generally are intimidated by them.

The passive consumers will be cooperative in general, but given their susceptibility to social influence, it is not wise to compose a study team of passive consumers and reticents only.

Active leadership and an active governance process will increase the influence of the social climate of the school and tend to pull faculty members toward more active states of growth. In the most affirmative climates, reticent personnel do not act out their jaundice by obstructing initiatives. In fact, a productive social climate is their best opportunity for growth.

Because collective activity generally requires coordinated activity among all personnel, differences in states of growth are critical as the faculty selects and follows directions for school improvement. The norm in many faculties (an unwritten, but powerful rule) has been to select directions and then allow those persons who do not want to participate "off the hook." The ostensible reason is that teaching styles are so different that collective action would interfere with the productive activities of some of the faculty. The real reasons are quite different. One is that collective activity has not been normative and many teachers are much more unclear about the role as faculty member than they are about the role as instructor. Collective components thus involve the establishment of some new norms. The other is that is the easiest-seeming course of action for dealing with the most passive consumers and the reticent personnel. Faculty after faculty has started school improvement activities with the volunteers and the hope that the initiative would spread as it was successful, only to discover that lateral diffusion does not work and, even more important, that collective initiatives with partial participation greatly weaken the initiative.

However, collective action is not dangerous to mental health, but rather the opposite. The governance process needs to emphasize the development of the affirmative climate where the energy released, and the benefits to the children, pull everyone into more active states of growth in the workplace. Essentially, positive climates have therapeutic benefits for all of us.

The Systemic Component

If we can assume that systemic initiatives are focused on a few objectives during any given time period, are well-coordinated, are the product of a collaborative governance system (chapters two, three and five), and have been thoroughly communicated, then the key to implementation becomes the development of a district-wide synergy that relates training and support to the schools where the implementation takes place. Individual differences in response will have parallels to those described in the discussions immediately above about the Individual and Collective Components. However, the size and complexity of the larger organization generate some additional considerations.

First, the success of system initiatives will depend partly on whether the central administration personnel, principals and other school-site leaders, and committee and council members behave like active consumers. They have to understand that the behavior patterns characterized by the higher states of growth are infectious and lead to the affirmative stances that facilitate problem solving. Mechanical processes of implementation simply are not effective. Leaders have to model the states of growth and affirmative stances toward the environment that they hope will be characterized by all personnel.

Second, the systemic initiatives need to be planned with increases in states of growth as an objective. Opportunities for growth are important. The social climate of the organization is the key, however, to capitalizing on those opportunities. Leaders and staff development personnel need to study the processes of building affirmative climates and involving people in collaborative governance processes and in conducting training and the study of content positively and richly.

We are what we eat, not just biologically but socially and emotionally. Rich substance, well-organized, in positive circumstances makes us richer, more outreaching, and more productive.

CHAPTER ELEVEN

BUYING TIME

The workplace of teachers was organized long before anyone anticipated that lifelong study and the careful preparation of learning environments would be necessary. Time to plan teaching or study it were not built into the schedule. Now we have to face the problem of arranging for the time for study groups and coaching teams to operate effectively.

The long-term way to provide time for staff development will be, of course, for the organization to employ teachers for an additional 20 or 30 days each year and to designate the additional time for developmental activities. In fact, we believe that teachers should be employed full time, that is, under 12-month contracts with provision for study and preparation made, then, a major part of the job. Here and there around the United States we can find districts that are moving in that direction. In March of 1987 the state legislature of Georgia passed legislation authorizing its education agencies to employ one-fifth of their teachers each year for the summer to study academic content, curriculum, and instruction. This is a start on the road to what we hope will be regular year-round employment for teachers.

We also have to recognize that most districts are not ready to go quite that far, and that time for training and for peer coaching needs to be developed within the constraints of the workplace as it now exists.

In the earlier chapters we have described the organization of training designed to give education personnel the opportunity to develop skill in models of teaching new to them and to transfer those models (sometimes called teaching strategies) into their active teaching repertoires (Joyce & Showers, 1983; Showers, 1985). We have argued that the evidence supports two working hypotheses on which training can reasonably be based. The first is that combinations of demonstrations, practice with feedback, and the study of the rationale of the strategy, if well executed, enable nearly all of us to develop an initial level of skill sufficient to shape teaching episodes around those models. The second is that the transfer of those models into the teaching repertoire so that they can be used powerfully and appropriately to increase student learning occurs during extensive practice in the classroom. For most persons, about 20 or 30 trials with the new model of teaching are needed until the skill matures to the point where a comfortable, flexible level of use is achieved. The transfer process is facilitated by the companionship of peers who help one another analyze teaching episodes and navigate the refinements that make the strategy a strong, smooth component of the teacher's professional repertoire. We have termed the companionship, with observation and formal and informal feedback to partners, a coaching relationship. Without coaching or a provision for its equivalent, very few education professionals practice new teaching strategies until they become part of the working repertoire.

Therefore, we recommend that staff development programs include demonstrations, opportunities for practice with feedback, and the study of the underlying theory of any new strategies that are the substance of the training. As initial skill is obtained, the participants should be organized into teams to implement the coaching component. Within the community of peer coaches, pairs of teachers (coaching partners) visit one another and discuss how to make the strategies work. Larger teams made up of several pairs meet regularly to share successes and discuss problems, watch demonstrations, and receive advanced instruction. Until we have developed alternatives (and we are trying to do so) peer coaching or the equivalent appears to be essential if the investment in training is not to be lost, a loss usually attended by a sense of disillusionment and frustration by trainers and trainees alike.

In most school settings a number of very practical problems have to be solved in order to provide the time for teachers to observe one another, discuss the model of teaching, and adapt it to their purposes and settings. These problems, of course, are products of defects in the workplace, principally that time either for preparation of teaching or for staff development is not an embedded feature of the work life of teachers. Thus the implementation of any sort of on-site follow-up to training (really the second stage of training) involves the development of conditions that are somewhat different from the traditions of the workplace. As it is put to us so often, "How can we provide time for coaching, both the observations and discussions of teaching?"

This chapter addresses that question and offers a set of suggestions for costless or low-cost ways of providing time for the implementation of peer coaching (and, incidentally, for other innovations requiring time). Each of the suggestions has been used in settings in the United States and Canada. Not all of them will be equally attractive to staff development personnel, administrators, or teachers, and not all of them can be used in any given setting, but taken together they provide avenues through which time for peer coaching can be arranged in nearly any setting.

Our objective is to come as close as possible to a situation where every teacher can observe another professional each week and discuss the teaching episode and be observed with appropriate discussion. For an elementary school of 20 teachers we are seeking about 20 hours each week, about one hour per teacher, to sustain a consistent coaching program. As we examine each of these ideas we will be concerned with how much of the need each can address.

1. *Administrators free teachers to observe by taking their classes.* In several schools with which we are familiar the principals teach about one period each day. The average ratio of building administrators to teachers is about 1-to-20. If each administrator taught one period per day, about one-fourth of the teachers would be released for a period each week. If supervisory personnel as well took a turn in the classroom on a daily or weekly basis, the benefits would be enlarged. Administrators alone, teaching one period a day, can provide about one-fourth of the hours we are looking for.

In addition, we believe that all school personnel who are not assigned to regular classroom teaching should substitute for another teacher at least one period each day. That includes guidance counselors, special education personnel, and personnel staffing other categorical programs. The work of such persons might well be enhanced by such a practice by enabling them to develop and demonstrate practices for serving the students. For example, resource specialists in special and bilingual education frequently support classroom teachers by helping them provide for students having special needs in classroom settings. By teaching regularly they could enable the teachers to observe them as they use the teaching strategies and other procedures designed for those children.

In a 40-teacher school with a principal, an assistant principal, a resource specialist, and a reading specialist we would reach half our goal if each worked regularly with a classroom-sized group.

2. *Larger than classroom size group instruction.* In most schools nearly all instruction is provided in classroom-sized groups of students. By bringing students together in larger groups teachers can be freed to visit one another.

In another school with which we are familiar one of the teachers is expert in the teaching of children's literature. She gathers half of the upper-grade students together for an hour and a half once a week for the study of a short story or a book, sometimes showing them films of that piece of literature. On other days she works with the other half of the upper-grade students and groups of primary students. She enjoys the work and is good at it, and brings important content to the children.

Literature is not the only subject that can be handled in large groups. Science, social studies, writing, art, music, and physical education are among the subjects that are amenable. We have seen quite a number of schools where pairs of teachers free one another regularly by teaching both classes in the subjects where they have greater strength or simply where the bringing together of two classes with one teacher is as efficient as when each teaches the same content to one classroom-size group.

Our literature teacher frees *every* teacher in the school for one hour and a half each week, easily meeting our objective by herself.

3. *Independent study and research.* Frequently instruction is followed by study, practice, and locating and assembling information. Often these activities can take place in a library or other setting as well or better than in the classroom.

We know an outstanding librarian who encourages teachers to use the library as a setting for independent study and will accept 60 students at any given time in addition to students who are there as individuals or small groups. She has four volunteer aides on duty at any given time to help provide service to the students and help check books in and out and return them to their shelves.

If every teacher took advantage of this opportunity only once each week, our goal would be achieved.

4. *Volunteer aides.* It has been well established that there are many adults in virtually every community who are willing if not eager to donate time to the school in the role of instructional aide. Some schools have recruited cadres of such persons to the extent that each teacher has a staff of two aides for a half-day each week. The presence of these persons enables a number of arrangements to be made that free teachers for peer coaching. Two of these have been mentioned above – larger than classroom-size group instruction and independent study, for the aides can provide attention to individuals and small groups.

Where teachers have aides in the magnitude that we recommend, it is not difficult to reach our goal.

5. *Student teachers.* Student teachers (and aides in some states) can be given limited certificates that permit them to have legal responsibility for students. We recommend that student teachers be placed in teams of two or more, because they can provide coaching to each other and also because they can more quickly reach the point of comfort in the classroom

where they can take over instructional episodes. For one or two periods each week they can take the class, experiencing a greater degree of independence than they feel when the teacher is present and freeing teachers to join their coaching teams.

6. *Team arrangements for teaching.* We have suggested above that teachers might be paired not only for coaching but for larger than classroom-sized instruction in areas where they have compensating competencies. Especially in the elementary school where teachers are asked to provide instruction in several content areas, pooling competencies can improve the quality of instruction. Where this is done, teachers quite easily can free one another to engage in the peer-coaching observation and discussions. Where the entire school employs such an arrangement, the entire program we envision can be implemented.

7. *The use of video.* The development of the Minicourses at the Far West Laboratory (Borg, Kelly, Langer, & Gall, 1970) demonstrated 15 years ago how effectively teachers can use videotape to study their teaching and practice teaching skills. Although live observation should not be completely replaced by taping, many coaching sessions can be carried out with its use.

We have visited several schools where the principal or someone else tapes teachers while they teach. The teacher and the coaching partner can then view the tape and discuss it. In several schools the entire faculty gathers to watch tapes (and live teaching episodes). This is not the worst use for part of the agenda of faculty meetings. Where television is used regularly, all faculty can study teaching one or more times each week.

SUMMARY

We believe that there are very few schools where several of these options cannot be implemented. If all of them were used simultaneously (which we would not recommend) our goal would be reached at least five or six times over.

If all else fails, paid substitutes can free teachers (about six per day for one period). However, we recommend that the costless options be tried first, because all of them provide potential educational benefits for the children. Resources for released time through substitutes should be reserved to free personnel for the vital components of training.

We are aware that circumstances in particular schools provide obstacles for each of our suggested arrangements in many settings. Some principals do not want to teach, or feel they are too busy. Some teachers do not want aides or student teachers. Some librarians are uncomfortable with more than a few students at a time or any students without the presence of another teacher.

Some districts provide aides with legal responsibility for students while others do not.

Most of these problems can be solved, but even where they are not, the options are so many that the general problem of time for coaching can be managed in nearly every school. Even a modest combination of several of these ideas can do the trick.

Also, in situations where coaching is not implemented on a school-wide basis, as when cadres of volunteers study models of teaching new to them and coach one another, any one of these suggestions, even used modestly, can provide time not only for coaching but for training as well.

CHAPTER TWELVE

MATTERS OF POLICY

Instead of writing a traditional summary chapter we decided that it was more appropriate to bring the substantive exposition of the book to a close with a focus on the process of policy making and to summarize the content in a series of recommended policies for school districts, intermediate agencies, and state and provincial departments of education.

The array of policies that govern activities in school districts emanate from many sources and are formulated in a variety of ways. Policy making is frequently envisioned as a process of formal debate that results in guidelines for action. And so it can be. However, decisions made in practice can become customs that have the force of policy. Also, formal policy decisions that run counter to customary behavior are more difficult to administer than those that fit in with the norms. Reflection about policy needs to take that into account.

Inevitably, some areas of institutional functioning have not been comprehensively submitted to a policy analysis because the areas were not brought to the attention of the policy-makers as needing thorough policy analysis. These areas are often characterized by collections of policies that apply to fragments of the area. In most school districts staff development is an area that has not been submitted to a comprehensive policy analysis. Yet many staff development activities occur and a large proportion of them are governed by specific policies or tradition. Federal, state, and local district initiatives are often created to accomplish specific purposes without attention to a comprehensive plan that is governed by a comprehensive policy. This practice is inevitable where comprehensive planning has not occurred.

CREATING POLICY IN A VACUUM:
THE EXPERIENCE IN SPECIAL EDUCATION

When Public Law 94-142 was passed and augmented in many cases by state legislation having the same intent—to provide services to students having special needs while providing that they will have education under the least restrictive and separative conditions—a substantial portion of the funds were allotted to the implementation of the program, including administration and staff development for teachers in both special education and regular classroom situations. Were it that all 17,000 school districts in the United States possessed comprehensive human resource development systems, the legislation could have directed that the staff development and other implementation resources be administered in coordination with the comprehensive system and its policies. Even if not so directed, the school districts could have brought together the directors of special education and the human resource development system and directed them to work out a coordinated plan to accomplish the legislative intent.

As it was, the personnel responsible for the implementation of this huge initiative needed to figure out what to do in the absence of policies ensuring coordination at the local level. A large amount of activity ensued of the following types.

State Intermediate Agencies

Some states established special regional centers to provide administrative support and staff development services or developed departments in existing offices in intermediate agencies or counties. These centers or departments designed staff development programs for special education personnel and regular classroom teachers. These programs competed for the attention of teachers and administrators with other initiatives from the federal, state, and local district levels.

Departments in Districts

Because of the large number of personnel supported by the special education authorizations, many local districts established central office departments of special education responsible for employing, placing, and coordinating special education teachers in neighborhood schools and centers offering special services. These departments were also responsible for managing the identification of students with special needs and ensuring that individual educational programs were prepared for those students.

In the first years following the legislation, the number of students identified as needing special needs approximately doubled, to about 15 percent of all students. In some districts the proportion reached one third or even higher.

The district departments generated staff development offerings for the personnel directly connected to them and for regular classroom teachers and administrators. Their services competed for the attention of those personnel and portions of the three to four days of yearly staff development allotted for most teachers by their districts.

Resource Teachers

A new category of teacher/helping teacher was established to provide services to children and for teachers while the mainstreaming effort was being accomplished. An excellent idea in principle, the resource-teacher concept has labored because the new personnel needed to be coordinated by principals who had no experience with such a role and little training about optimal utilization. Also, the new teachers themselves were inexperienced in staff development roles, had little or no training for the function, and often were much younger than the teachers they were expected to help. In many cases they ended up developing and providing pull-out programs for students, an arrangement easy to administer and which avoided the stress of trying to operate staff development programs for their more experienced and in some cases suspicious colleagues.

Policy and Coordination

The enormous initiatives to attempt to integrate students with special needs funded under PL 94-142 and the correlated state legislation represented an attempt to bring about a substantial change in education practices. For most districts, coordinating an innovation of that size and complexity was probably about as much of a systemic initiative as the organization could sustain for a period of perhaps two to four years. Optimally it should have been accompanied by substantial amounts of staff development for principals, supervisors, regular teachers, and the new special education personnel in matters ranging from special education program design, options for mainstreaming, skills for working with students and skills for working with one another in a coordinated fashion.

In most settings, however, it had to compete with numerous other initiatives that were operating at the same time and its training programs have had to work their way into schedules already packed with activities. Hence, this most moral and important initiative has struggled, adding to the proliferation of pull-out programs. These programs fragment the curriculum for so many students today and aggravate the regular teachers who have difficulty maintaining continuity with an ever-changing population of students.

After we have visited the questions of policy for comprehensive staff development programs, we will return to the case of special education and examine how the scenario might be different were a comprehensive policy in force.

POLICY ISSUES AND QUESTIONS

In the next few pages we will present a series of questions that policy-makers might ask themselves at state, regional, and district levels as the emerging human resource system is developed. Who are these policy-makers? Certainly they include the cabinet of the district or other agencies – the highest executive body – and the school board or trustees of the district or agency. They are the members of the district (or regional or state) staff development council as we described it in the earlier chapters, with representatives of the cabinet, board, and schools. The director of staff development in the agency should be a member of the district cabinet. Initiatives by other personnel or departments are critically dependent on staff development and executive coordination is essential if they are to succeed.

What are the questions these policy-makers need to ask themselves to create an effective human resource development system and, in the interim, a strong and well-coordinated staff development program?

Is a Long-term Goal of the Agency the Development of a Comprehensive Human Resource Development System? This question requires careful consideration and a realistic assessment of current capability and budgets, current programs, and study of the options. The content of the first 10 chapters or the equivalent should be, we believe, available to the policy-makers as they consider this question.

An assessment needs to be made of the extent to which the current programs in the district address the needs of individuals, schools, and system initiatives, the extent to which they are directed toward content that promises to help students grow, and the nature of the current training and the likelihood that it will result in transfer to practice.

In the process of making this assessment, all sources of offerings for staff development should be considered. In one district we worked with recently, we found that the staff development program was considered to be the offerings by a two-person staff development department. In fact, other units in the district—a curriculum department, departments of elementary and secondary education, bilingual education, equality of educational opportunity, computer science, and over 30 other units were sponsoring programs, let alone the substantial offerings of the local universities.

Will the Establishment of a Comprehensive Human Resource Development System be Treated as an Innovation? As we have described the potential content and processes of training in just a few possible areas (chapters four to eight) it is probably apparent that a comprehensive system is in itself an innovation. Few current programs include the training elements that ensure transfer. Most schools have a way to go before they reach the state of synergistic cooperation described in chapter three. Few trainers have conducted the types of training we have described. Many teachers are unaccustomed to working together. Some have escaped anything above the minimum of required training for many years. Many district departments are accustomed to independence, rather than coordination under a systemic umbrella. Personnel have become accustomed to weak implementation of systemic initiatives. Cooperative governance is a novelty in some situations. Collective decision making is an innovation in many schools.

Innovations are sustained only when there are thorough vertical and horizontal understandings throughout the organization (Fullan, 1982) and with careful and systematic training of all personnel involved and the careful phasing-in of elements of the innovation.

Thus, another formulation of the question is: "What will be the nature of the plan for bringing about this innovation in the agency?"

Will a Governance/Communication Structure be Established to Provide for the Identification of Program Elements for the Clinical, Collective, and Systemic Components? In chapters two, three and five we described various aspects of a system of governance that provides for coordination at the cabinet level and the organization of all system personnel in teams, study groups, councils, and committees that can consider program options in all three substantive components and the support components.

The systems for governance are also processes for communication. While there is no reason why everyone cannot have access to the decision-making process, all people in a large organization cannot have their own way, and the decisions that are made need to be communicated to everyone not only in terms of what will be done by others but what is their part in the process.

This is a more radical innovation in most systems than many people realize. As decisions are made for the structures and processes for governance and communication, it needs to be recognized that putting them in place will require extensive coordination and in many cases a reorientation of administrators and teachers. For example, as shocking as it is to report, we have encountered building administrators in some settings who actually believe that part of their job is to *protect* their faculty from communication and initiation from the district office. For those persons a major reorientation is required when a coordinated effort is introduced by the agency.   For those central office personnel who have operated initiatives separately from their colleagues in other departments, extensive processes will be necessary, with leadership from the superintendent and deputies, to build a cooperative environment as devoid of turf-protective behavior as possible.

What Provisions will be made to Develop a Synergistic Organizational Climate in the Schools? We have stressed throughout the importance of the climate of the individual school. A comprehensive system will depend greatly on the ability of principals and building administration teams to create a collaborative climate in which faculty, administration, and community members both study the health of the school and create the collective components of the system, but also the conditions for the implementation of effective training for individuals and the support of systemic initiatives.

For many building administrators, facilitation of the creation of a synergistic environment requires fresh perspectives and skills. Any formula for organizing the staff in the ways we describe in chapters two and three will require process skills that may have to be generated in programs for those administrators.

To What Extent will the System Endeavor to Select Options that Promise to Increase Student Learning in the Academic, Social, and Personal Domains? We have argued throughout, particularly in chapters four and five, that there is a substantial reservoir of potential staff development content that offers the opportunity for increased student development and would constitute new repertoire for most education personnel. If the governance/communication system is properly organized, these options can be studied and made known as decision making is generated.   An affirmative answer to the question raised above is a commitment to orienting district policy to include the best available knowledge in all district practices and a willingness to challenge conventional wisdom when policy is implemented.   Vague promises of an undetermined magnitude will go by the wayside.

We assert that very large gains in student learning and aptitude can be achieved if current knowledge is employed, and we expect future research to generate even more powerful options.

For the present, we favor the goal-setting enunciated by Bloom (1984) when he suggests that we should strive to make instruction in schools as effective as if each student had his own full-time tutor. If we do that, achievement will change by such a magnitude that nearly half of the students will achieve more than the best students do now, the average student will achieve what the 90th percentile student does now, and the students in the bottom decile will be achieving what students in the normal range do now. We believe that the common understanding that the students have much greater aptitude than has been revealed by normal practice should be the driving force in the system. Whether the agency policy-makers believe this will have much to do with the commitment they will have to the possibilities of a human resource development system. When school personnel ask us, "But how do you convince the board members that staff development is important?" we suggest using the plain facts about the potential for student learning.

Will Staff Development Programs be Designed to Ensure that a High Degree of Mastery of Skills and Knowledge Results? Another way of putting this is to ask whether research on training will be used for program design. The research is clear. Teachers are very capable learners. If they have the chance to study the rationale of an approach to teaching, see an adequate number of demonstrations, and have opportunities to practice and receive accurate feedback about performance, nearly all can master a wide range of teaching skills and academic knowledge.

Current programs can be improved quickly if those training elements are arranged appropriately.

A commitment to this policy also implies that some district personnel need to be organized into a cadre that can deliver training incorporating those elements.

Will Training Include Provision to Ensure Practice and Implementation of those Skills into Active Practice? Again, the research is remarkably clear. The companionable coaching process, where teachers help each other with the process of innovation, greatly increases the incidence of implementation.

A failure to provide follow-up to training as a part of training virtually ensures that transfer will not take place.

However, the development of coaching teams without adequate training in the content will have no effect.

Will Time for the Study of Teaching and Coaching be Embedded into the Workplace? Nearly all the building administrators we have worked with have needed information about how to arrange time costlessly or nearly without cost (see chapter eleven). The implementation of effective training will have little effect without the organization of study groups and peer coaching teams. Similarly, they cannot function without the smooth provision of time. A few simple arrangements can provide the two or three hours each week that is needed without hindering the instructional program. District policy needs to cover this subject and principals will need the information and support necessary to make the arrangements.

Will Evaluation Reveal the Extent to Which New Skills and Content are Used and the Effects on Student Behavior and Achievement? If the answer is affirmative a considerable innovation in the evaluation of staff development events will occur. Opinionaires about the attractiveness of training and its perceived usefulness are the norm as this is written. The procedures described in chapter nine enable a much clearer assessment of impact (Hall, 1986).

A COMMITMENT TO LEARNING HOW TO DO THE JOB

If all of the questions above are answered in the affirmative, a significant change will occur in the commitment of central office personnel, staff development providers, and council and committee members to study the process of staff development itself. Learning how to organize faculties, developing the skill to implement effective training, engaging in the process of decision making based on knowledge about what works require study and practice, and more study and practice. We are talking about a big innovation in education, one that will change all of us.

CHAPTER THIRTEEN

THE INITIAL PREPARATION OF TEACHERS

Staff development and preservice teacher preparation bear a reciprocal relationship to one another. Each borrows strength from the other. If preservice teacher education is strong, continuing education has more to build on. If continuing education is strong, preservice education can be designed with confidence that life-long learning can take place. In a field such as education, where there is a struggle for professional status, the reciprocal relationship is of particular importance, for professionalization is a product of the initial and continuing education of its personnel.

In the embrace of education, a professional community is built. Its members share the conceptions of knowledge and skill that distinguish the profession and the language for communicating and applying them in the workplace. We are in the early stages of a movement to attempt to restructure teacher education to the point where teaching can achieve a defensible level of professionalization. Currently preservice education is very weak and the development of a vigorous human resource development system is just beginning. Neither can build a professional community unless they are drastically extended and reorganized around agreed-on knowledge and skills. Whether a reform can be achieved depends heavily on the definition of the common core of professional content – a consensus that has eluded us in the past. However, this may be the time; the signs are fairly good. The volume of criticism of teacher education and schooling has not abated but there is a more healthy component of proposals for improvement. Goodlad, Adler, Smith, and others are offering solutions as well as identifying problems (see Joyce & Clift, 1984). In addition, there is an increasingly serious literature about the nature of professional knowledge and skill (e.g., Gideonse, 1982; Judge, 1982).

Also, some important changes are occurring in the length of programs and the nature of the student body. Programs are getting longer, making it easier to do justice to both the liberal and technical components, and some programs have become more selective. Initiatives for reform are also coming from a balance of sources in both the United States and Canada. Federal agencies and figures, even persons as prominent as former vice-president Mondale, are urging changes. Provincial ministries and state departments of education are searching for the basis for more effective programs. Organizations of teachers (Rauth, Biles, Billups, & Veitch, 1983) and teacher educators are moving toward consideration of structural reforms. Researchers (Brophy, Berliner, Shulman, Hall) are seeking ways of shortening the distance between knowledge production and educational practice and AERA has established a division of teaching and teacher education. Innovations in teacher education that go beyond those that can be accomplished through administration (length and selection are two examples) but also require changes in substance, process, and structure will not be easy to bring about, but the range of persons and agencies advocating extensive changes augurs well. The climate is propitious. Although there are many major dimensions of the teacher education reform problem, unless a strong consensus is developed about the nature of professional knowledge and skills, a reform that ensures the professionalization of the education professions will not be achieved. To capitalize on the favorable climate we need to build a conceptual framework on which we can reconstruct the substance, process, and structure of teacher education. We need to find a consensus about the nature of professional teaching, one that can guide common reform while encouraging well-grounded innovators to develop and test new ideas and researchers to expand and solidify the knowledge base. The framework needs to be communicable to the diverse populations that have to think and work together to bring about sweeping reform. Government officials, accrediting and certifying agencies, university officials, education and arts and science faculties, public school personnel, teacher candidates, and interested citizens have to be able to talk the same language and support wide-scale changes. (Teacher education is the business of many interested parties.) A coalition of ideas and people will have to be forged to sustain the magnitude of reform that is needed.

A MATTER OF ETHOS

The core of reform will be a conception of the nature of professional behavior. We believe that unless reforms are linked to a basic idea about professional behavior in education, the results will be largely cosmetic and fragmentary, based on pragmatic and ad hoc, rather than fundamental, concerns.

Fullan's (1982) position that for an institution to sustain substantial reform requires a shared and deep understanding about the nature of the reform is our guide here. We believe that all of us interested in teacher-education reform have to share an understanding of the major tenets of professional behavior. Without that common conception we are unlikely to stand the stress of reform and find the costs of giving up our customary behavior worth the benefits of improved performance. In the case of teacher education the core ideas are conceptions of the nature of professional behavior. Our major business is to bring about a change in the ethos of the profession, building it around understandings about the nature of professional skill and how it can be acquired. These ideas need to lift the conception of professional behavior from a pragmatic survival orientation to one that envisions teaching as an artful use of carefully-accumulated evidence about effective practices, evidence drawn from both clinical observation and research. To achieve and disseminate such a synthesis is within our grasp, thanks to the considerable advances in technologies for accumulating evidence and media for disseminating them.

However, the development of a community of educators that can base practice on a combination of scientific and clinical knowledge involves a social change of considerable magnitude (Joyce & Clift, 1983), in fact, the creation of an ethos of professional practice radically different from the one that presently exists. First of all, current teaching and schooling practices are rarely knowledge based. Teachers and administrators alike have not been prepared to understand the research base, to design practices based on it, or to accumulate and share clinical knowledge. Teacher and administrator preparation suffers from the lack of a framework that defines professional problems and links them to formal or informal knowledge about solutions. In fact, many practitioners are skeptical about knowledge-based practice. They learned their craft in the classroom and built their separate knowledges about how to conduct practice. Many feel that the mediators of research (their professors) deserted them at a time of great need – their first days of teaching. Most know a good deal about teaching but their understandings are not communicated or leavened by the knowledge of others. Further, teachers live under five conditions that mitigate against the development of collective and reflective practice. First, they work alone, for the most part, in the cellular structure of the school (Lortie, 1975). Second, the loosely-coupled components of educational organizations disconnect the work of teachers from one another and that of administrators. Concerted organizational action is rare. Third, teaching was originally conceived as a reflexive activity that could be done with minimal preparation. Time to prepare for teaching was not built into the assignment of the teacher. The reflective consideration of alternatives requires time to examine problems and consider the various solutions to them. A work life that requires action without much time for preparation is not conducive to complex decision making.

Fourth, time for collective decision making is essential for the reflective design of curriculums and school environments. Such time is also not built into the work time of teachers. Meetings for teams of teachers, school faculties, and district organizations is hard to come by. If groups of professionals are to absorb knowledge and plan to use it, time for collective work has to be made available. Finally, time and the opportunity for the study of academic substance and educational process is essential if teachers and administrators are to keep abreast of progress and develop the skills to utilize new knowledge as it develops. The teacher and administrator have to be regular students of education, academic substance, and the emerging trends and events of the social world of the nation and planet.

As one talks with practitioners in other fields, the contrast between their lives and those of teachers is arresting. The dental unit that cares for the authors is an interesting example. The hygienist, who is in charge of the cleanliness of our teeth and the health of our gums, recently planned a trip to Russia – offered by the professional organization, time off paid by the clinic – in which seminars on her specialty are interspersed with what she calls "my opportunity to exchange ideas on practice in our countries." When we were in India recently, we made a number of videotapes demonstrating the responses of Indian children to North American teaching strategies. Although teachers are interested in the children's reactions, many teacher educators have told us that the Indian experience is not relevant to the needs of the American classroom. Not so our dental hygienist. She thinks that understanding the world is somehow relevant – that cross-cultural understanding will enhance her performance. Part of the complexity of reform in teacher education derives from the ethos that has been created by the present workplace of educators and reform in teacher education has to include some changes in that workplace if it is to be effective. Particularly, the following changes have to be made:

1. Inservice education has to be increased dramatically. We cannot build a knowledge-based teacher education without assuming that the knowledge base will be increased over the period of service (potentially 30 to 50 years). For the study of academic substance, educational process, and world affairs, teachers need a life-long link to universities and other sources of study. Further, training needs to be provided that is adequate

to allow the development of the skills that permit knowledge to be translated into practice (Joyce & Showers, 1983).

2. If knowledge is to inform practice, time for planning its use needs to be provided in the workplace of the teacher and administrator. There is little use in orienting teachers to the existence of alternative curriculums without giving them time to study the alternatives and make decisions about how to use them.

Finally, collaborative decision making is essential not only to collective action, but to the development of a community that engages in the study of practice. Altogether, then, we are addressing the problem of the development of an ethos of professional practice – a world-wide community of educators who are closely linked to the formal knowledge base and who, on a local level, study the effects of their own practice and communicate it to their colleagues.

The Knowledge Base

It would be difficult to build an ethos around a knowledge base were it woefully inadequate. In chapter four we examined four promising lines of inquiry that are in search of effective teaching.

We are encouraged by our analysis. All four lines of inquiry are promising. Each has been able to generate descriptions of teaching skills that have potential as definitions of professional behavior, and thus, as objectives of teacher education. The skills range from good practices that will get effects but require little training to practices that require complex knowledge and interactive skill acquired only through extensive training and long practice. The naturalistic studies provide practices that promise to improve classroom teaching by a series of small but significant modifications of normal practices. Some of these improvements can be made with little training but others appear to require more extensive training and a few of the important ones (like carrying on instruction or lesson development) require further definition.

The theory-driven line has produced descriptions of complex skills in both the cognitive and interactive domains of teaching that have great promise for increasing the effects of instruction but also require extensive training and practice. While some models have very specific purposes (as skill in the analysis of social issues), many increase the general effects of schooling. Nondirective, cooperative, and inductive methods generally increase student learning of information and concepts as well as the achievement of the particular objectives toward which they are directed (attitudes toward

self, intergroup relations, the process skills of science). Curriculum research
has achieved very large effects in some cases and the skills include mastery of
academic substance as well as the theory of the curriculum and the
interactive skills and logistical ability to implement the curriculum. Extensive
training and practice are required. The effective schools research has
generated the skills of working as a faculty to produce productive social
climates. The skills of creating an effective school are very complex and
include social process skills, the ability to think through the mission of the
school, and the skills necessary to create and implement strong and coherent
curriculums. In addition, it appears that school improvement depends
greatly on the ability of the faculty to create the conditions that are favorable
for productive innovation, including the setting for intensive and extensive
self-training (Joyce & Showers, 1983; Showers, 1984). In addition, the
leadership skills identified by Fullan (1982) and Leithwood and Montgomery
(1982) are required of the administrative staff. The important question is
whether we have a sufficient base of research to define many of the objectives
of preservice programs around researched skills. We think so. Similarly,
the base will support the orientation of inservice programs to enable teachers
to acquire and use these skills and to generate the school climate that
increases learning and the likelihood that tested innovations can be
implemented in the workplace of educators. Most of the skills that emerge
from the research are generic. That is, with modification they are applicable
across grades and subjects and educational settings (learning centers,
resource-based programs, and classrooms).

Four categories of research-based skills can be assembled for preservice
and inservice applications. Each has contributed some understanding of the
skills in the categories that are represented. Management skills refer to the
behaviors that stabilize the instructional situation and induce students to stay
busy with tasks that are monitored and adjusted to their progress. Models of
teaching are, in terms of skill, the ability to use research-based educational
environments to increase learning of various kinds. Curriculum skills are
those required to implement research-based curriculums in schools so that
academic substance and instructional process are coherently organized and
have a cumulative impact.

School climate skills are those required to create a learning community
where the social organization generates energy and rewards individual and
collective effort toward excellence in achievement and cooperation. The
skills of school improvement may well lie at the core. The research from
all four lines of inquiry, but especially the research on models of teaching,
curriculum, and school improvement, indicates that using the research to

teacher has to have the skills for acquiring teaching skills – and the skill to create a climate in the school that is favorable to innovation.

Learning How to Learn

All the skills identified by the research require modifications in present practice. Learning how to learn may well be the key skill – the one that unlocks the door to using research to improve school practice.

Perhaps the most important finding from the last 10 years of research on training is how dramatically teachers improve their skills in learning once they are given the opportunity to practice learning complex teaching skills and strategies.

Thus, in addition to introducing teacher candidates to the knowledge base that can inform practice and enabling them to develop a solid initial repertoire of teaching skills and strategies, teacher education programs can be constructed to enable its students to become more effective learners.

States of Growth

Teacher education institutions have the opportunity to have a great influence on the social and intellectual tone of the student body. Also, although what they will teach and how they will teach it will greatly affect their students for several decades, possibly their most pervasive and enduring influence will be from their roles as models of what human beings should be. In subtle as well as obvious ways, the ideals they embody will be communicated to their students. If teachers are outreaching, seeking persons, confident of their place in the world and their ability to interact productively with their environment, they will communicate with their presence the richness of human potential. If they are passive, they will model and thus teach passivity. If they are reticent, they will teach their students fear of the world.

Teacher education can be constructed to increase the states of growth of its students who become the teachers of states of growth for the thousands of students they will contact in their careers.

SUMMARY

Thus, our message about teacher education is relatively simple. It should be oriented toward the re-creation of the ethos of the education profession-in-the-making. As such it should introduce its students to the knowledge base that can undergird and sustain practice. It should employ the best knowledge that is known about training, modeling the use of research on education, and enabling its students to become powerful learners. It can be designed to induce its students toward high states of growth, for their own sake and that of the people they will be asked to teach.

CODA

A MATTER OF WILL

Generally speaking, this is a technical book. We have described the outline of a possible human resource development system in education and discussed its purpose. We have suggested a system for selecting content for it and for designing training. We have discussed a system for thinking about individual differences and a plan for adjusting the system to make it productive for a wide spectrum of people and making affirmative stances toward the environment (high states of growth) a major objective. We have discussed evaluation and a plan for relating preservice and inservice programs conceptually and practically.

Technical feasibility, however, will not suffice to fuel a major innovation within this enormous system of education. Ultimately, the development of a strong and responsive system for staff development and school improvement will depend on aspiration for the educational system and the will to see those aspirations realized.

Thus our closing words are more spiritual than they are technical. They come from our own aspirations and love for children and those who teach them.

We begin by sharing one of the moving experiences we have had in a small school in the Far East.

A SCHOOL OF INSPIRING ASPIRATIONS

About 30 miles from Delhi, India, on the road that leads to the Punjab, there is a school at the edge of the village of Rai. It is named the Motilal Nehru School of Sports. Rai is in the state of Haryana, whose legislature established the school in 1972.

Much of Haryana's population lives in villages whose rhythmic pattern of life has been little changed for hundreds of years. In the mists of the early

167

morning the women gather at the well, helping each other to draw water and heave the filled earthen pots onto their heads. Groups of children head into the fields where the water buffalo have been grazing, gathering the fresh dung and patting it into cakes that are stacked to dry for use as cooking fuel. The morning bells of the Ashram gently mark the first religious observances of the day, and the chants of the monks murmur across the fields. If a visitor looks closely, the ragged front edges of the modernization that is to come can just be discerned. Electric lines have reached a few houses, although the current is not yet strong or reliable enough to support the television sets that will soon influence the villagers' perceptions of the world. Rubber tires are appearing on the wheels of the more elaborate ox carts and the flocks of cattle belonging to the leading ashrams are sprinkled with new breeding stock. An occasional auto or truck is in residence among the oxen and camels. And, in each of these villages there is a school. In most there is a blackboard and in a few there are enough textbooks to go around.

Each winter the teachers of the villages and cities of Haryana are asked to nominate their most promising eight-year old boys and girls as candidates for the school at Rai. The ones whose parents agree (many will not, especially the parents of females) journey to Rai and are given tests to measure their academic aptitude. Those who excel will be invited back and given tests of physical aptitude. Those who perform best are invited to attend the school. They will live for 10 years on a 500-acre campus with clothes, food, books, and other supplies provided by the state. (There is a small fee for the children of the wealthy.) In addition to dormitories, classrooms, library, infirmary, dining halls, and auditorium, the inventory of facilities includes stadia for cricket and swimming; a gymnasium equipped primarily for gymnastics; soccer and hockey fields; tennis, basketball, volleyball, and squash courts; and housing for the faculty and maintenance staff.

The curriculum for the youngest children is reminiscent of a fine American suburban school. The chief differences are that instruction occurs in both Hindi and English and the curriculum includes greater attention to athletics, the arts, and the sciences.

At about age 11 the pace quickens for the students. The daily schedule is generally as follows:

0530-0700 *Socially Useful and Productive Work* The children assist in maintaining the grounds, help out in an orphanage on the edge of the campus, and work on a variety of projects designed to enhance the campus. These projects include weaving, painting, crafting lamps and other appliances, and, most dramatically, participating in the construction of facilities. Last year the students did much of the physical work involved in building an outdoor, Greek-style theater large enough to accommodate the entire student body.

0700-0800 *Breakfast.*

0800-1300 *Academic Instruction.* Included are language and literature, science, social studies, art, and music. Some days include an assembly in which the older students give talks in both English and Hindi — talks designed to be both informative and amusing.

1300-1500 *Lunch and Personal Time.*

1500-1730 *Athletic Training.* The students select the sports they will concentrate on.

1730-2200 *Personal and Study Time.* Some evenings there are films or theatrical presentations.

This schedule is maintained for five and one-half days each week. Saturday afternoon is reserved for personal and study time, informal sports, and often a film or theatrical presentation is scheduled.

The structure of the schedule is the direct embodiment of the missions of the school. The physical campus concretely symbolizes them in the beauty of the grounds, the sculpture of the classrooms, library, and stadia, and the growing facilities in whose construction the students have such an intimate role. The missions are symbolized also in the office of the director. Its aesthetic furnishings — hangings, rugs, reproductions of sculptures and trophies — softly speak their piece. Behind his desk is an array of four pictures that convey a less subtle message. It carves its way into one's consciousness. For there, flanking the conventional pictures of Pandit Nehru and Mahatma Gandhi, are the likenesses of Karl Marx and Abraham Lincoln, their profiles turned slightly toward each other across the founders of the Indian nation. When the visitors manage to inquire how these four happen to be together, the director rumbles, as if it should be obvious, "Because they are all gentlemen." After a pause to see if his audience can decipher that message for themselves, he continues, "Each of them had their egos and the need to serve their societies in balance. Their personal ambition and drive found its fruition in their ability to contribute in a basic way to their own people and all the peoples of the world. They enhanced themselves through giving and could give so much because they became enlarged as people."

It takes some weeks of walking the campus, watching the classes, chatting with the very cheerful and earnest students, playing with them and the faculty, and dealing with their well-reasoned and passionate arguments in classrooms, dormitories, gardens, and auditorium, before it becomes clear how pervasively the meaning of the director's words is enacted in the manifest and tacit curriculums of the school. In the more familiar jargon of our trade the missions of the school are three:

First, that the students shall be dedicated to the improvement of the Indian society and those of their brothers and sisters throughout the world.

Second, that they will be able to navigate successfully the environments of both Indian and foreign universities, garnering the fruits of scholarly life for themselves and their people.

Third, that they will strive to develop their bodies until they can represent their nation in international competition in athletics.

All this is aspired for the fewer than 800 students of this little school. And these are the goals for all the children — each is to strive in all three domains. A close examination of life in the villages that spawn these children underlines the complete outrageousness of these missions. The current cliche' about Third World education puts it rather nicely: "They are being propelled from the age of the bullock cart to the space age in just 10 years." From villages where the leading families are desperately frustrated as they try to communicate to their fellow citizens about the nature of the pollution in the wells, these children emerge to head for medical school, space engineering, and to invent new and better computers.

Although they were selected from the fastest learners and swiftest runners of their primary schools, most of them at the time of their admission to the school would be labelled culturally-disadvantaged in American society, or at least the society of our schools. They would be perceived to have very limited life experience, at least of the kind that makes for success in today's world. And it is with dismay that the visitor realizes that, in many of America's school, they would have been consigned to a world of low expectations. In the optimistic and demanding environment of the School for Sports, the transformation of the intellectual life of these children is so rapid and so complete that the faculty of the school have come to regard their growth as commonplace and unremarkable. Their concern is less that the school is so powerful in changing the children's intellectual and social perspectives and so effective in helping them actualize their potential than that the transformation may be too rapid. "Will the children lose their roots?" they wonder, "Will they lose the spirituality that graces their villages and become infatuated with the lures of technology, intellectualism, and materialism? Will they turn inward and use their talents only for their personal gain?" That they can achieve the academic transformation of their students, however, the staff have no doubt. They perceive the children to be fortunate rather than remarkable.

While the school is ambitious in all domains, from a technical point of view the athletic mission is the most unlikely one in which to have such confidence. The village environment does not expose the students to the sports they will attempt to master at the school. Neither formal nor sand lot sports are available. The types of exercise the students have at home are not the kinds we associate with athletic prowess. As we observe these students running and jumping in their tests of athletic ability we are not reminded of American city children racing around the corner or playing stickball, nor our children of the beaches, delicately flipping a frisbee or powerfully diving under a wave. Most of the children who enter the Motilal Nehru School of Sports are rather slow and awkward by American standards. That is why we say that it is in the athletic domain that the staff harbors the most impossible of their dreams. Precisely because of that, we are reminded that what is important about educational aspirations is not a belief that our students have the aptitude and prior development that makes high achievement likely but rather that it is through effort and aspiration that aptitude is developed and great achievement is made. To know that you can develop is more important than to believe that you are excellent by birth or background. There, we believe, is the nub of the lesson from the Motilal Nehru School of Sports. In an impoverished state in a nation tortured by all manner of economic, social, and political problems, they have created a school that believes that talent can be developed – that schools can not only capitalize on the abilities students bring with them but can develop aptitude as well.

Returning home to America, we have been inspired by the lofty goals and determination of not only the little school at Rai but also several others that seek difficult objectives. Noteworthy was an elementary school for urban shantytown girls in Pune that persuades the parents to permit the young women to attend school by arranging half-time work for them as domestics so they can contribute to the family income while getting their education. A rural cooperative near Kolhapur operates a farm designed to teach agriculture to the citizens of all ages, a supermarket designed to teach consumer education, a sugar refinery that provides a market for the local cane and a paper mill that turns the by-products into high quality paper. The entire cooperative is a continuing education center. It also harbors a school whose aspirations rival those at Rai, except in the athletic domain.

THE AMERICAN ATTITUDE

Back in America, we were more than a little troubled by some of the attitudes we found in our favored nation. A woman from Scotland reminded us recently of the old story that all-seeing deities realize that they have to create two heavens, one for Americans and one for the rest of the world, because Americans have a "glass-half-full" mentality that diminishes advantages and magnifies imperfections. There is some justification for this bit of irony. As we listen to many of our colleagues and citizens we sometimes feel we are listening to a litany of despair in the midst of the most favored conditions in the world. We are especially struck by talk suggesting that we are

helpless — that there are good and valid reasons why we cannot reach many of our students.
A number of complaints come easily to mind.

- *Class size.* We hear about the too-large numbers of children in our classes. ("There's nothing we can do with these hordes of children.") The other day we heard a lot of that genre of comment from a staff of 80 that works with a student body of just 1,500!
- *Teacher fatigue.* We hear about burned-out personnel. ("We can't expect much from this aging staff.") Last month during a workshop a principal said to us, "I'm 45 now, and getting along toward retirement. What incentives can be provided to people of my age to engage in the kind of energetic school improvement efforts you are talking about?" (We wondered how Lee Iacocca would have responded to that question.)
- *Teacher ability.* We hear a lot of talk about teacher ability. ("Not enough bright people come into education" (Vance & Schlecty, 1982). We hear little talk about our well-educated and gifted teachers.
- *The conditions of teaching.* We hear about how the conditions of the workplace make teachers lose the will to teach (McLaughlin, 1986) and little about the conditions that enable faculties to work together to innovate and adapt ideas from their colleagues (Fullan, 1982; Leithwood & Montgomery, 1982).
- *Inadequate research.* Some members of the research community appear to deprecate the research on effective schools (Rowen, Bossert, & Dwyer, 1983; Purkey & Smith, 1983). Granting the design problems in that difficult line of research, do those researchers really believe that a positive social climate does not benefit student learning? As Gage has pointed out so eloquently (1978) we have often, as a corollary to our quite reasonable effort to avoid making Type A errors, not so reasonably been guilty of rather massive Type B errors and underestimated what has been learned (especially by others.)
- *Family background.* We hear so much talk about the poor family backgrounds of students that we are beginning to think that people really believe Coleman's peculiar assertion that schools and teachers don't make a difference (Coleman et al., 1966, Jencks et al., 1972). Apparently many practitioners and researchers agree with this position, which portrays educators as powerless because the socioeconomic background of the students is conceived to be of such overwhelming importance. We wonder why we hear so little about the research of Spaulding (1970) and others who have demonstrated how much we can raise student aptitude and achievement.

- *Parental neglect.* Talk about student background is also frequently accompanied by talk about family disinterest in school. ("If the parents don't care, what can we do?") We wonder why we don't hear more about programs such as the Urban-Rural school development program and its outstanding success in involving parents in the education of their children (Joyce, 1978).
- *Learning styles.* After a lifetime of the study of learning styles we never thought we'd be distressed by the subject, but we are upset by the direction discussion about individual differences has taken. ("This child can't learn from lectures because she is right-brained. That one can't write creatively because he is left-brained. This one is really bright but has this immobilizing learning disability.")

We should probably cut our list of peeves short at this point and just mention our surprise that anyone seriously believes that this generation is the first to be distracted by drugs and sex, or that the peer culture was recently invented.

Why, instead, are we not hearing more about the efforts of Pressley, Levin, Delaney (1982) and their associates, who have developed ways of helping children master information from two to four times faster than usual? Or the substantial achievements in making presentations using Advance Organizers (Lawton & Wanska, 1977)? Or the success with inductive methods of teaching science, including effects on tests of aptitude (Bredderman, 1983)?

A bare mention of the constant complaints about lack of money will suffice.

Do we detect a malaise or are we imagining things? Have Americans forgotten how favored we are and how much we have achieved and, more important, can achieve? Are we challenged by the incredible achievement of Japanese children in some subject areas (Walberg, 1985, reported that by grade six the American and Japanese class average distributions no longer overlap on mathematics achievement tests) and the performance of Asian immigrants to the United States or are we sinking into a sump of helplessness and excuses? We have been surprised by how casually teachers dismiss the Japanese success ("It kills their creativity.") or, accepting it, turn again to our old friend, family background and interest, as the cause. (Do our teachers really believe that American parents have lost interest in education?)

We are reluctantly coming to the conclusion that American educators greatly underestimate the effect that schools can have on learners, either ignore or are ignorant of the really fine achievements in recent educational research and how to implement it, and greatly magnify the problems of personnel, resources, and organization.

We believe, and think our belief is warranted, that schools can have a powerful and lasting effect on children and we have the knowledge and resources to do the job if we will just shake off our malaise and get to work. As Benjamin Bloom (1981) has pointed out, it makes sense to stop worrying about the "unmalleable" variables (we can't resplice anyone's genes) and concentrate on the malleable ones. Perhaps what is most important is to realize that we have attributed unmalleability to a great many variables that we can in fact influence. The school can, in fact, teach students how to learn, can provide background at virtually any stage in life, and can help students use their individual differences rather than letting them sink under their liabilities. Teachers can learn at any age and, in fact, it has been demonstrated that they can learn just about any teaching strategy and how to implement just about any curriculum (Joyce & Showers, 1983).

We are inspired by schools like the Motilal Nehru School of Sports because those people just don't seem to know when they are licked. They do not psych themselves out of the game. And they succeed for the simplest of reasons — because students can learn and schools can teach. At this point in history we do not begin to know just how much children can learn or how powerful education can become. But, at its best today, education is powerful and we need to believe that, because it is true.

The creation of human resource systems both depends on affirmative views of human existence and the potential of the human spirit. Education is not just a business and teaching is not just a vocation or a profession. As teachers we hold our children and their future in the cradle of our hands and we need to accept that condition seriously without being overwhelmed. Successful teaching and the successful teaching of teachers depends on the cockeyed optimists' view of human potential.

Quite simply, it is unlimited by anything except our own vision.

REFERENCES

Almy, Millie (1970). *Logical thinking in the second grade.* New York: Teachers College Press.

Anderson, Harold & Brewer, Helen (1939). Domination and social integration in the behavior of kindergarten children and teachers. *Genetic Psychology Monograph, 21, 287-385.*

Anderson, L., Evertson, C., & Brophy, J. (1979). An experimental study of effective teaching in first grade reading groups. *Elementary School Journal, 79,* 193-223.

Aspy, David N., Roebuck, Flora, Willson, M., & Adams, O. (1974). *Interpersonal skills training for teachers.* (Interim report #2 for NIMH Grant #5PO 1MH 19871.) Monroe, LA: Northeast Louisiana University.

Atkinson, R. (1975). Nemotechnics in second language learning. *American Psychologist, 30,* 821-828.

Ausubel, David (1963). *The psychology of meaningful verbal learning.* New York: Grune and Stratton, Inc.

Baker, Robert G. & Showers, Beverly (1984). *The effects of a coaching strategy on teachers' transfer of training to classroom practice: A six-month followup study.* Paper presented at the annual meeting of the American Educational Research Association, New Orleans, LA.

Baldridge, Victor & Deal, Terrence (1975). *Managing change in educational organizations.* Berkeley: McCutchan.

Ball, S. & Bogatz, G. A. (1970). *The first year of Sesame Street.* Princeton, NJ: Educational Testing Service.

Barnes, B. & Clawson, E. (1975). Do advance organizers facilitate learning? Recommendations for further research based on an analysis of 32 studies. *Review of Educational Research, 45* (4), 637-659.

Becker, Wesley & Gersten, Russell (1982). A followup of Follow Through: the later effects of the direct instruction model on children in the fifth and sixth grades. *American Educational Research Journal, 19* (1), 75-92.

Bennett, Barrie (1987). *The effectiveness of staff development training practices: a meta-analysis.* Ph.D. thesis, University of Oregon.

Bentzen, M. (1974). *Changing schools: The magic feather principle.* New York: McGraw-Hill.

Berman, Paul & McLaughlin, Milbrey (1975). *Federal programs supporting educational change, Vol. IV: The findings in review.* Santa Monica, CA: The Rand Corporation.

Bloom, B. S. (1984). 2-sigma problem:The search for methods of group instruction as effective as one-to-one tutoring.: *Educational Researcher, 13* (6), 4-16.

Bloom, B. S. (1981). *The new direction in educational research and measurement: Alterable variables.* Paper presented at the annual meeting of the American Educational Research Association, Los Angeles, CA.

Boocock, Sareen & Schild, E. (1968). *Simulation games in learning.* Beverly Hills: Sage Publications, Inc.

Borg, W. R., Kallenbach, W., Morris, M., & Friebel, A. (1969). Videotape feedback and microteaching in a teacher training model. *Journal of Experimental Research, 37,* 9-16.

Borg, W. R., Kelley, Langer, P., & Gall, M. (1970). *The Minicourse.* Beverley Hills, California: Collier-Macmillan.

Bredderman, Ted (1983). Effects of activity-based elementary science on student outcomes: A quantitative synthesis. *Review of Educational Research, 53* (4), 499-518.

Brookover, Wilbur, Schweitzer, J., Schneider, J., Beady, C., Flood, P., & Wisenbaker, J. (1978). Elementary school social climate and school achievement. *American Educational Research Journal, 15* (2), 301-318.

Brophy, Jere & Evertson, Carolyn (1974). *The Texas teacher effectiveness project: Presentation of non-linear relationships and summary discussion.* Austin, TX: Research and Development Center for Teacher Education, University of Texas.

Brophy, Jere & Good, Thomas (1986). Teacher behavior and student achievement. In Merlin Wittrock (Ed.), *Handbook of Research on Teaching, 3rd Edition,* pp. 328-375. New York: Macmillan Publishing Co.

Bruner, Jerome (1961). *The process of education.* Cambridge, MA: Harvard University Press.

Chamberlin, C. & Chamberlin, Enid (1943). *Did they succeed in college?* New York: Harper and Row.

Clark, Christopher & Peterson, Penelope (1986). Teachers thought processes. In Merlin Wittrock (Ed.), *Handbook of Research on Teaching,* pp. 225-296. New York: Macmillan Publishing Co.

Clark, Christopher & Yinger, Robert (1979). *Three studies of teacher planning* (Research Series #55). East Lansing: Michigan State University.

Coleman, James, Campbell, E., Hobson, C., McPortland, J., Mood, A., Weinfield, E., & York, R. (1966). *Equality of educational opportunity.* Washington, DC: Government Printing Office.

Collins, K. (1969). The importance of strong confrontation in an inquiry model of teaching. *School Science and Mathematics, 69* (7), 615-617.

Collins Standard Dictionary (1978). New Delhi: Oxford and IBH Publishing Co.

Costa, Arthur (1985). *Developing minds: A resource book for teaching thinking.* Alexandria, VA: Association for Supervision and Curriculum Development.

Crandall, David, et al. (1982). *People, policies, and practices: Examining the chain of school improvement.* Vols. I-X. Andover, MA: The NETWORK, Inc.

Crawford, J., Gage, N., Corno, L., Stayrook, N., Mittman, A., Schunk, D., Stallings, J., Baskin, E., Harvey, P., Austin, D., Cronin, D., & Newman, R. (1978). *An experiment on teacher effectiveness and parent-assisted instruction in the third grade.* (3 vols.) Stanford, CA: Center for Educational Research at Stanford, Stanford University.

Dalton, Michael (1986). *The thought processes of teachers when practicing two models of teaching.* Ph.D. Thesis, University of Oregon.

Dalton, Michael & Dodd, Jennifer (1986). *Teacher thinking: The development of skill in using two models of teaching and model-relevant thinking.* Paper presented at the annual meetings of the American Educational Research Association, San Francisco.

Devaney, Kathy & Thorn, L. (1975). *Exploring teacher centers.* San Francisco: Far West Laboratory for Educational Research and Development.

Dewey, John (1916). *Democracy in education.* New York: Macmillan, Inc.

Dewey, John (1937). *Experience in education.* New York: Macmillan, Inc.

Dunn, Rita & Dunn, Kenneth (1975). *Educator's self-teaching guide to individualizing instructional programs.* West Nyack, NY: Parker.

Edmonds, Ronald (1979). Some schools work and more can. *Social Policy, 9* (5), 28-32.

Elefant, Emily (1980). Deaf children in an inquiry training program. *The Volta Review, 82,* 271-279.

El Nemr, M. (1979). *Meta-analysis of the outcomes of teaching biology as inquiry.* Ph. D. thesis, University of Colorado.

Erikson, Erik (1950). *Childhood and society.* New York: Norton.

Evertson, C., Anderson, C., Anderson, L., & Brophy, J. (1980). Relationships between classroom behaviors and student outcomes in junior high mathematics and English classes. *American Educational Research Journal, 17* (1), 43-60.

Feeley, Theodore (1972). *The concept of inquiry in the social studies.* Ph.D. thesis, Stanford University.

Fisher, C., Berliner, D., Philby, N., Marliave, R., Cahen, L., & Dishaw, M. (1980). Teaching behaviors, academic learning time, and student achievement: An overview. In C. Denham and A. Lieberman (Eds.) *Time to learn.* Washington, DC: National Institute of Education.

Flanders, Ned (1970). *Analyzing teacher behavior.* Reading, MA: Addison-Wesley.

Fullan, Michael (1982). *The meaning of educational change.* New York: Teachers College Press.

Fullan, Michael, Miles, Matthew, & Taylor, Gib (1980). Organization development in schools: the state of the art. *Review of Educational Research, 50* (1), 121-84.

Fullan, Michael & Park, Paul (1981). *Curriculum implementation: A resource booklet.* Toronto: Ontario Ministry of Education.

Fullan, Michael & Pomfret, Alan (1977). Research on curriculum and instruction implementation. *Review of Educational Research, 47* (2), 335-397.

Gage, N. L. (1963). Paradigms for research on teaching. In N. L. Gage (Ed.) *Handbook of research on teaching,* pp. 94-141. Chicago: Rand McNally & Company.

Gage, N. L. (1978). *The scientific basis for the art of teaching.* New York: Teachers College Press.

Gall, Meredith & Gall, Joyce (1976). The discussion method. *The Psychology of Teaching Methods.* The seventy-fifth yearbook of the National Society for the Study of Education. Chicago: University of Chicago Press, pp. 166-216.

Gall, Meredith, Haisley, Faye, Baker, Robert, & Perez, Miguel (1982). *The relationship between inservice education practices and effectiveness of basic skills instruction.* Eugene, OR: Center for Educational Policy and Management, University of Oregon.

Gideonse, H. D. (1982). The necessary revolution in teacher education. *Phi Delta Kappan, 64* (1), 15-18.

Good, Thomas, Grouws, Douglas, & Ebmeier, Howard (1983). *Active mathematics teaching.* New York: Longman, Inc.

Goodlad, John (1984). *A place called school.* New York: McGraw-Hill.

Goodlad, John & Klein, Frances (1970). *Looking behind the classroom door.* Worthington, OH: Charles A. Jones.

Gordon, William J. J. & Poze, Tony (1971). *The metaphorical way of learning and knowing.* Cambridge: Porpoise Books.

Gregorc, A. F. (1982). *An adult's guide to style.* Maynard, MA: Gabriel Systems.

Griffin, Gary, Ed. (1983). *Staff Development.* Eighty-second yearbook of the National Society for the Study of Education. Chicago: University of Chicago Press.

Guskey, Thomas (1986). Staff development and the process of change. *Educational Researcher, 15* (5), 5-12.

Hall, Gene (1986). *Skills derived from studies of the implementation of innovations in education.* A paper presented at the annual meetings of the American Educational Research Association, San Francisco.

Hall, Gene & Loucks, Susan (1977). A developmental model for determining whether the treatment is actually implemented. *American Educational Research Journal, 14* (3), 263-276.

Halpin, A. W. (1966). *Theory and research in administration.* New York: Macmillan.

Harvey, O.J., Hunt, David, & Schroeder, Harold (1961). *Conceptual systems and personality organization.* New York: John Wiley and Sons, Inc.

Hoetker, James & Ahlbrand, William (1969). The persistence of the recitation. *American Educational Research Journal, 6,* 145-167.

Howey, Kenneth, Yarger, Sam, & Joyce, Bruce (1978). *Improving teacher education.* Washington: Association for Teacher Education.

Hunt, David (1971). *Matching models in education.* Toronto: Ontario Institute for Studies in Education.

Hunt, D. E., Butler, L. F., Noy, J. E., and Rosser, M. E. (1978). *Assessing conceptual level by the paragraph completion method.* Toronto: Ontario Institute for Studies in Education.

Hunt, David & Joyce, Bruce (1967). Teacher trainee personality and initial teaching style. *American Educational Research Journal, 4,* 253-259.

Hunter, Madeline (1980). Six types of supervisory conferences. *Educational Leadership, 37,* 408-412.

Hunter, Madeline & Russell, D. (1981). Planning for effective instruction: Lesson design. In *Increasing your teaching effectiveness.* Palo Alto, CA: Learning Institute.

Ivany, George (1969). The assessment of verbal inquiry in elementary school science. *Science Education, 53* (4), 287-293.

Jackson, Phil (1966). *The way teaching is.* Washington: National Education Association.

Jencks, C., Smith, M., Acland, H., Bane, M. J., Cohen, D., Gintis, H., Hayns, B., & Michelsohn, S. (1972). *Inequality: A reassessment of the effect of family and schooling in America.* New York: Basic Books.

Johnson, David & Johnson, Roger (1975). *Learning together and alone.* Englewood Cliffs, NJ: Prentice Hall, Inc.

Johnson, David & Johnson, Roger (1979). Conflict in the classroom: Controversy in learning. *Review of Educational Research, 49* (1), 51-70.

Johnson, David & Johnson, Roger (1981). Effects of cooperative and individualistic learning experiences on inter-ethnic interaction. *Journal of Educational Psychology, 73* (3), 444-449.

Johnson, David, Maruyama, G., Johnson, Roger, Nelson, D., & Skon, L. (1981). Effects of cooperative, competitive, and individualistic goal structures on achievement: a meta-analysis. *Psychological Bulletin, 89* (1), 47-62.

Joyce, Bruce (1978-79). Toward a theory of information processing in teaching. *Educational Research Quarterly, 3* (4), 66-77.

Joyce, Bruce (Ed.) (1978). *Involvement: A study of shared governance of teacher education.* Washington, DC: ERIC Clearinghouse on Teacher Education.

Joyce, Bruce (1980). *Teacher innovator system: Observer's manual.* Eugene, OR: Booksend Laboratories.

Joyce, Bruce (1987). Essential reform in teacher education. In Linda Newton, Michael Fullan, and John W. MacDonald (Eds.), *Rethinking Teacher Education,* pp. 1-27. Toronto: Ontario Institute for Studies in Education.

Joyce, Bruce, Bush, Robert & McKibbin, Michael (1982). The California Staff Development Study. *The January 1982 Report.* Palo Alto: Booksend Laboratories.

Joyce, Bruce & Clift, Renee (1983). *Generic training problems: Training elements, socialization, contextual variables, and personality disposition across occupational categories that vary in ethos.* Paper presented at the annual meetings of the American Educational Research Association, Montreal.

Joyce, Bruce & Clift, Renee (1984). The phoenix agenda: Essential reform in teacher education. *Educational Researcher, 13* (4), 5-18.

Joyce, Bruce & Harootunian, Berj (1967). *The structure of teaching.* Chicago: Science Research Associates.

Joyce, Bruce, Hersh, Richard, & McKibbin, Michael (1983). *The structure of school improvement.* New York: Longman.

Joyce, Bruce, McKibbin, Michael, & Bush, Robert (1984). *Predicting whether an innovation will be implemented: four case studies.* Paper presented at the annual meetings of the American Educational Research Association, New Orleans.

Joyce, Bruce, Peck, Lucy, & Brown, Clark (1981). *Flexibility in teaching.* New York: Longman, Inc.

Joyce, Bruce & Showers, Beverly (1983). *Power in staff development through research on training.* Washington: Association for Supervision and Curriculum Development.

Joyce, Bruce & Showers, Beverly (1986). *Peer coaching guides.* Eugene, OR: Booksend Laboratories.

Joyce, Bruce, Showers, Beverly, Beaton, Colin & Dalton, Michael (1984). *Teaching skills derived from naturalistic and persuasion-oriented studies of teaching: A comparison of results.* Paper presented at the annual meeting of the American Educational Research Association, New Orleans.

Joyce, Bruce, Showers, Beverly, Dalton, Michael & Beaton, Colin (1985). *Theory-driven and naturalistic research as sources of teaching skills:* A classification. Paper presented at the annual meeting of the American Educational Research Association, Chicago.

Joyce, Bruce & Weil, Marsha (1986). *Models of teaching.* Englewood Cliffs: Prentice-Hall, Inc.

Judge, H. G. (1982). *American graduate schools of education: A view from abroad.* New York: Ford Foundation.

Kerman, Sam (1979). Teacher expectations and student achievement. *Phi Delta Kappan, 60* (10), 716-718.

Knowles, Malcolm (1978). *The adult learner: A neglected species* (2nd ed.). Houston: Gulf Publishing Co.

Lara, Anunciacion V. & Medley, Donald M. (1987). Effective teacher behavior as a function of learner ability. *Professional School Psychology, 2* (1), 15-23.

Lawton, J. T. & Wanska, S. (1977). Advance organizers as a teaching strategy: A reply to Barnes and Clawson. *Review of Educational Research, 47* (1), 233-244.

Leithwood, Kenneth & Montgomery, Donald (1982). The role of the elementary school principal in program improvement. *Review of Educational Research, 52,* 309-339.

Levin, Joel, Shriberg, L., & Berry, J. (1983). A concrete strategy for remembering abstract prose. *American Educational Research Journal, 20* (2), 277-290.

Little, Judith Warren (1982). Norms of collegiality and experimentation: Workplace conditions of school success. *American Educational Research Journal, 19* (3), 325-340.

Lortie, Dan (1975). *Schoolteacher.* Chicago: The University of Chicago Press.

Loucks, S. F., Newlove, B. W., & Hall, G. E. (1975). *Measuring levels of use of the innovation: A manual for trainers, interviewers, and raters.* Austin: Research and Development Center for Teacher Education, The University of Texas.

Luiten, J., Ames, W. & Ackerson, G. (1980). A meta-analysis of the effects of advance organizers on learning and retention. *American Educational Research Journal, 17* (2), 211-218.

McCarthy, Bernice (1981). *The 4mat system: teaching to learning styles with right/left mode techniques.* Barrington, Ill.: Excel, Incorporated.

McDonald, Fred & Elias, Patricia (1976). *Executive summary report: beginning teacher evaluation study, phase two.* Princeton, NJ: Educational Testing Service.

McKibbin, Michael & Joyce, Bruce (1980). Psychological states and staff development. *Theory into Practice, 19* (4), 248- 255.

McLaughlin, Milbrey, Pfeifer, R. Scott, Swanson-Owens, Deborah, and Yee, Sylvia (1986). Why teachers won't teach. *Phi Delta Kappan, 67* (6), 420-426.

McNair, Kathleen (1978-1979). Capturing in-flight decisions. *Educational Research Quarterly, 3* (4), 26-42.

Marzano, Robert, Brandt, Ron, Hughes, Carolyn, Jones, Beau , Presseisen, Barbara, Rankin, Stuart, & Suhor, Charles (1987). *Dimensions of Thinking.* Alexandria, VA: Association for Supervision and Curriculum Development.

Maslow, Abraham (1962). *Toward a psychology of being.* New York: Van Nostrand.

Medley, Donald (1977). *Teacher competence and teacher effectiveness.* Washington, DC: American Association of Colleges of Teacher Education.

Medley, D. M., Coker, H., Coker, J. G., Lorentz, J. L., Soar, R. S., & Spaulding, R. L. (1981). Assessing teacher performance from observed competency indicators defined by classroom teachers. *Journal of Educational Research, 74,* 197-216.

Medley, Donald & Mitzel, Harold (1958). A technique for measuring classroom behavior. *Journal of Educational Psychology, 49,* 86-92.

Medley, Donald & Mitzel, Harold (1963). Measuring classroom behavior by systematic observation. In N. L. Gage (Ed.) *Handbook of Research on Teaching,* pp. 247-328. Chicago: Rand McNally and Co.

Medley, Donald, Soar, Robert & Coker, Homer (1984). *Measurement- based evaluation of teacher performance.* New York: Longman.

Miles, Matthew & Huberman, Michael (1984). *Innovation up close.* New York: Praeger.

Myers, Isabel Briggs (1962). *The Myers-Briggs type indicator.* Palo Alto, CA: Consulting Psychologists Press.

National Institutes of Education (1975). *National conference on studies in teaching, Vols. 1-10.* Washington, DC: U.S. Department of Health, Education and Welfare.

Nelson, J. (1971). *Collegial supervision in multi-unit schools.* Ph.D. Thesis, University of Oregon.

The New Oxford Illustrated Dictionary (1978). Oxford: Systems Publications Limited in Association with Bay Books and Oxford University Press.

New Webster's Dictionary of the English Language (Deluxe Encyclopedia Edition) (1981). United States of America: Delair Publishing Co., Inc.

Perkins, D. N. (1984). Creativity by design. *Educational Leadership, 42* (1), 18-25.

Peterson, Penelope & Clark, Christopher (1978). Teachers reports of their cognitive processes while teaching. *American Educational Research Journal, 15,* 555-565.

Peterson, Penelope, Marx, Ronald, & Clark, Christopher (1978). Teacher planning, teacher behavior, and student achievement. *American Educational Research Journal, 15,* 417-432.

Phi Delta Kappa (1983). *Improving your own instruction: Self-assessment and peer review.* Bloomington, IN: Phi Delta Kappa.

Phi Delta Kappa (1985). *Exemplary practice series.* Bloomington, IN: Phi Delta Kappa.

Pressley, Michael (1977). Children's use of the keyword method to learn simple Spanish vocabulary words. *Journal of Educational Psychology. 69* (5), 465-472.

Pressley, Michael & Dennis-Rounds, J. (1980). Transfer of a mnemonic keyword strategy at two age levels. *Journal of Educational Psychology, 72* (4), 575-582.

Pressley, Michael, Levin, Joel, and Delaney, H. (1982). The mnemonic keyword method. *Review of Educational Research, 52* (1), 61-91.

Pressley, Michael, Levin, Joel, & Ghatala, E. (1984). Memory-strategy monitoring in adults and children. *Journal of Verbal Learning and Verbal Behavior, 23* (2), 270-288.

Pressley, Michael, Levin, Joel, & McCormick, C. (1980). Young children's learning of foreign language vocabulary: A sentence-variation of the keyword method. *Contemporary Educational Psychology, 5* (1), 22-29.

Pressley, Michael, Levin, Joel, & Miller, George (1981a). How does the keyword method affect vocabulary, comprehension, and usage? *Reading Research Quarterly, 16 ,* 213-226.

Pressley, Michael, Levin, Joel, & Miller, George (1981b). The keyword method and children's learning of foreign vocabulary with abstract meanings. *Canadian Psychology, 35* (3), 283-287.

Pressley, Michael, Samuel, J., Hershey, M., Bishop, S., & Dickinson, D. (1981). Use of a mnemonic technique to teach young children foreign-language vocabulary. *Contemporary Educational Psychology, 6,* 110-116.

Purkey, Stewart & Smith, M. (1983). Effective schools: A review. *Elementary School Journal, 83* (4), 427-452.

Ralph, J. & Fennessey, J. (1983). Science or reform: Some questions about the effective schools model. *Phi Delta Kappan, 64* (10), 689-694.

Rauth, M., Biles, B., Billups, L., & Veitch, S. (1983). *Educational research and dissemination program.* Washington, DC: American Federation of Teachers.

Rhine, W. Ray (Ed.) (1981). *Making schools more effective: New directions from Follow Through.* New York: Academic Press.

Ripple, R. & Drinkwater, D. (1981). Transfer of learning. In H.E. Mitzel (Ed.) *Encyclopedia of Educational Research,* Vol. 4, pp. 1947-1953. New York: The Free Press, Macmillan Publishing Company.

Roebuck, Flora, Buhler, J., & Aspy, David (1976). A comparison of high and low levels of human teaching/learning: Conditions on *the subsequent achievement of students identified as having learning difficulties.* (Final report: Order PLD6816-76 The National Institute of Mental Health.) Denton, TX: Texas Women's University Press.

Rogers, Carl (1961). *On becoming a person.* Boston: Houghton-Mifflin.

Rogers, Carl (1982). *Freedom to learn in the eighties.* Columbus: Charles E. Merrill.

Rolheiser-Bennett, Carol (1986). *Four models of teaching: A meta-analysis of student outcomes.* Ph.D. thesis, University of Oregon.

Roper, Susan, Deal, Terence, & Dornbusch, Sandy (1976). Collegial evaluation of classroom teaching: Does it work? *Educational Research Quarterly,* Spring, 56-66.

Rosenshine, Barak (1971). *Teaching behaviours and student achievement.* London: National Foundation for Educational Research.

Rowe, M. B. (1969). Science, soul and sanctions. *Science and Children, 6* (6), 11-13.

Rowe, M. B. (1974). Wait-time and rewards as instructional variables, their influence on language, logic, and fate control. *Journal of Research in Science Teaching, 11,* 81-94.

Rowen, B., Bossert, S. T., & Dwyer, D. C. (1983). Research on effective schools: A cautionary note. *Educational Researcher, 12* (4), 24-31.

Rutter, M., Maughan, R., Mortimer, P., Oustin, J., & Smith, A. (1979). *Fifteen thousand hours: Secondary schools and their effects on children.* Cambridge, MA: Harvard University Press.

Schiffer, Judith (1980). *School renewal through staff development.* New York: Teachers College Press.

Schmuck, Richard, Runkel, Philip, Arends, Jane, & Arends, Richard (1977). *The second handbook of organizational development in schools.* Palo Alto: Mayfield Press.

Schrenker, G. (1976). *The effects of an inquiry-development program on elementary school children's science learning.* Ph.D. thesis, New York University.

Schwab, Joseph (1965). *Biological sciences curriculum study:* Biology teachers' handbook. New York: John Wiley and Sons, Inc.

Schwab, Joseph (1982). *Science, curriculum, and liberal education: Selected essays.* Chicago: University of Chicago Press.

Schwab, Joseph & Brandwein, Paul (1962). *The teaching of science.* Cambridge, MA: Harvard University Press.

Sharan, Shlomo (1980). Cooperative learning in small groups: Recent methods and effects on achievement, attitudes, and ethnic relations. *Review of Educational Research, 50* (2), 241-271.

Sharan, Shlomo & Hertz-Lazarowitz, Rachel (1980). A group investigation method of cooperative learning in the classroom. In Shlomo Sharan, P. Hare, C. Webb, R. Hertz-Lazarowitz (Eds.), *Cooperation in Education,* pp. 14-46. Provo, UT: Brigham Young University Press.

Sharan, Shlomo & Hertz-Lazarowitz, Rachel (1982). Effects of aninstructional change program on teachers' behavior, attitudes, and perceptions. *The Journal of Applied Behavioral Science, 18* (2), 185-201.

Shavelson, Richard & Dempsey-Atwood, M. (1976). Generalizability of measures of teacher behavior. *Review of Educational Research, 46* (4), 553-611.

Shaver, James, Davis, O.L., & Helburn, S. W. (1978). *An interpretive report on the status of pre-college social studies education based on three NIE-funded studies.* Washington, DC: National Council for the Social Studies.

Showers, Beverly (1980). *Self-efficacy as a predictor of teacher participation in school decision-making.* Ph.D. thesis, Stanford University.

Showers, Beverly (1982). *Transfer of training: The contribution of coaching.* Eugene, OR: Center for Educational Policy and Management.

Showers, Beverly (1984). *Peer coaching: A strategy for facilitating transfer of training.* Eugene, OR: Center for Educational Policy and Management.

Showers, Beverly (1985). Teachers coaching teachers. *Educational Leadership, 42* (7), 43-49.

Sirotnik, Kenneth (1983). What you see is what you get: Consistency, persistence, and mediocrity in classrooms. Harvard Educational Review, 53 (1), 16-31.

Slavin, Robert (1983). *Cooperative learning.* New York: Longman, Inc.

Slavin, Robert (1986). The Napa evaluation of Madeline Hunter's ITIP: Lessons learned. *The Elementary School Journal, 87* (2), 165-171.

Smith, Karl & Smith, Mary (1966). *Cybernetic principles of learning and educational design.* New York: Holt, Rinehart, and Winston.

Smith, M. L. (1980). *Effects of aesthetics education on basic skills learning.* Boulder, CO: Laboratory of Educational Research, University of Colorado.

Snow, Richard (1982). *Intelligence, motivation, and academic work.* Paper presented for a symposium on "The student's role in learning," conducted by the National Commission for Excellence in Education, U.S. Department of Education, San Diego, California.

Soar, Robert (1973). *Follow Through classroom process measurement and pupil growth.* (1970-71 final report.) Gainesville, FL: Institute for the Development of Human Resources, University of Florida.

Soar, R. S., Soar, R. M. & Ragosta, M. (1971). *Florida climate and control system: observer's manual.* Gainesville, FL: Institute for Development of Human Resources, University of Florida.

Spaulding, Robert (1970). *Educational Improvement Program.* Durham, NC: Duke University Press.

Spaulding, Robert (1974). *CASES Manual.* San Jose: San Jose State University.

Spaulding, Robert (1978). *STARS Manual.* San Jose: San Jose State University

SRI International (1981). *Evaluation of the implementation of public law*

94-142. Menlo Park, CA: SRI International.

Stallings, Jane (1979). *How to change the process of teaching reading in secondary schools.* Menlo Park, Ca.: SRI International.

Stallings, Jane & Kaskowitz, D. (1972-73). *Follow Through classroom observation evaluation.* Menlo Park, CA: SRI International.

Stallings, Jane, Needels, Peggy, & Stayrook, Nick (1979). *The teaching of basic reading skills in secondary schools, Phase two and phase three.* Menlo Park, CA: SRI International.

Sternberg, Robert (1986). *Intelligence applied: Understanding and increasing your intellectual skills.* San Diego: Harcourt Brace Jovanovich.

Sternberg, Robert & Bahna, Kastoor (1986). Synthesis of research on the effectiveness of intellectual skills programs: Snake-oil remedies or miracle cures? *Educational Leadership, 44* (2), 60-67.

Stone, C. (1983). A meta-analysis of advance organizer studies. *Journal of Experimental Education, 51* (4), 194-199.

Suchman, Richard (1964). Studies in inquiry training. In R. Ripple and V. Bookcastle (Eds.) *Piaget reconsidered.* Ithaca, NY: Cornell University Press.

Taba, Hilda (1966). *Teaching strategies and cognitive functioning in elementary school children.* (Cooperative Research Project 2404.) San Francisco: San Francisco State College.

Thelan, Herbert (1960). *Education and the human quest.* New York: Harper and Row.

Thelan, Herbert (1967). *Classroom grouping for teachability.* New York: John Wiley and Sons, Inc.

Tobin, Kenneth (1986). Effects of teacher wait time on discourse characteristics in mathematics and language arts classes. *American Educational Research Journal, 23* (2), 191-200.

U.S. Department of Education (1986). *What works: Research about teaching and learning.* Washington: U.S. Department of Education.

Vance, V. S. & Schlechty, P. C. (1982). The distribution of academic ability in the teaching force: Policy implications. *Phi Delta Kappan, 64* (1), 22-27.

Voss, B. (1982). *Summary of research in science education.* Columbus, OH: ERIC Clearinghouse for Science, Mathematics, and Environmental Education.

Walberg, Herbert (1985). Why Japanese educational productivity excels. Paper presented at the annual meetings of the American Educational Research Association, Chicago.

Walberg, Herbert (1986). What works in a nation still at risk. *Educational Leadership, 44* (1), 7-11.

Wallace, R. C., Young, J. R., Johnston, J., Bickel, W. E., & LeMahieu, P. G. (1984). Secondary educational renewal in Pittsburgh. *Educational Leadership, 41* (6), 73-77.

Weil, Marsha, Marshalek, B., Mittman, A., Murphy, J., Hallinger, P., & Pruyn, J. (1984). *Effective and typical schools: How different are they?* Paper presented at the annual meeting of the American Educational Research Association, New Orleans.

Weiss, I. R. (1978). *Nineteen seventy-seven national survey of science, social science, and mathematics education.* National Science Foundation. Washington, DC: U.S. Governmant Printing Office.

White, W. A. T. (1986). *The effects of direct instruction in special education: A meta-analysis.* Ph.D. thesis, University of Oregon.

Wolpe, J. & Lazarus, A. (1966). *Behavior therapy techniques: A guide to the treatment of neuroses.* Oxford: Pergamon Press, Inc.

Worthen, Blaine (1968). A study of discovery and expository presentation: Implications for teaching. *Journal of Teacher Education, 19* , 223-242.

Zumwalt, Karen, Ed. (1986). *Improving teaching:* 1986 Yearbook of the Association for Supervision and Curriculum Development. Washington: Association for Supervision and Curriculum Development.

INDEX